Cambridge Elements ☰

Elements in Ancient East Asia
ENVIRONMENTS: Interaction Zones of Ancient East Asia
edited by
Erica Fox Brindley
Pennsylvania State University
Rowan Kimon Flad
Harvard University

ENVIRONMENTAL FOUNDATIONS TO THE RISE OF EARLY CIVILISATIONS IN CHINA

Yijie Zhuang
University College London

CAMBRIDGE
UNIVERSITY PRESS

Shaftesbury Road, Cambridge CB2 8EA, United Kingdom

One Liberty Plaza, 20th Floor, New York, NY 10006, USA

477 Williamstown Road, Port Melbourne, VIC 3207, Australia

314–321, 3rd Floor, Plot 3, Splendor Forum, Jasola District Centre, New Delhi – 110025, India

103 Penang Road, #05–06/07, Visioncrest Commercial, Singapore 238467

Cambridge University Press is part of Cambridge University Press & Assessment, a department of the University of Cambridge.

We share the University's mission to contribute to society through the pursuit of education, learning and research at the highest international levels of excellence.

www.cambridge.org
Information on this title: www.cambridge.org/9781009507424

DOI: 10.1017/9781009158954

First published 2024

A catalogue record for this publication is available from the British Library.

ISBN 978-1-009-50742-4 Hardback
ISBN 978-1-009-15896-1 Paperback
ISSN 2632-7325 (online)
ISSN 2632-7317 (print)

Additional resources for this publication at: www.cambridge.org/Yijie

Environmental Foundations to the Rise of Early Civilisations in China

Elements in Ancient East Asia

DOI: 10.1017/9781009158954
First published online: December 2024

Yijie Zhuang
University College London
Author for correspondence: Yijie Zhuang, y.zhuang@ucl.ac.uk

Abstract: The transition from the middle to late Holocene (5,000–4,000 BP) coincided with profound socioeconomic transformations and intensified regional and trans-regional interactions in late prehistoric China. These environmental and socioeconomic changes gave rise to diverse lifeways and settlement modes that constituted the foundation for the emergence of regional civilisations. In this Element, prehistoric China is divided roughly into the Highlands, Lowlands, and Coastal areas, each with unique environmental and ecological conditions and distinctive technological and economic traditions between 5,000–4,000BP. The author gathers and reviews large amounts of environmental and archaeological data, and reconstructs brief environmental and settlement changes and lifeways. The author argues that environmental conditions and subsistence adaptations are two of the engines driving the increased socioeconomic complexity and rise of civilisations in late prehistoric China. This title is also available as Open Access on Cambridge Core.

Keywords: environmental change, late-Holocene climate, late prehistoric China, Chinese civilisations

ISBNs: 9781009507424 (HB), 9781009158961 (PB), 9781009158954 (OC)
ISSNs: 2632-7325 (online), 2632-7317 (print)

Contents

Environmental Foundations to the Rise of Early Civilisations in China

Yijie Zhuang, UCL Institute of Archaeology

Data Sources

Most of the DEM data were from NASA Earth Observation Data, www.earth data.nasa.gov

Remote sensing data were from the Sentinel Satellite as part of the Copernicus Programme, http://sentinel.esa.int

Hydrology data were from National Earth System Data Center, www.geodata.cn

The settlement distribution data were mainly from the Atlas of Cultural Relics of each province published by the National Cultural Heritage Administration and Hosner et al. (2016).

Chronological Division of Different Holocene Eras

Early Holocene: 11,000–8,000BP

Middle Holocene: 8,000–4,000BP

Late Holocene: 4,000BP–present

Chronological Table of late-prehistoric cultures in different regions

Region			Culture	Date (cal.BP)
Highlands	Qinghai-Tibetan Plateau	Qinghai	Zongri culture Qijia culture	5,600–4,200 4,200–3,600
		Tibet	Karuo culture (and Qugong culture)	5,300–4,000 4,000–3,500
	Hexi Corridor and He-Huang Valleys		Majiayao phase Banshan phase Machang phase Qijia culture Siba culture	5,300–4,500 4,500–4,300 4,300–4,000 4,200–3,600 3,900–3,500
	Hetao Plain Jin-Shaan Plateau		Ashan-III culture Laohushan culture Longshan culture	5,000–4,500 4,600–4,300 4,300–3,800
	Fen-Wei Basin		Mid-Late Yangshao culture Miaodigou-II Longshan culture	6,000–4,700 4,700–4,300 4,300–3,800

Lowlands	Circum-Songshan Mountain and Luoyang Basin		Mid-Late Yangshao culture	5,900–4,500
			Miaodigou-II	4,500–4,300
			Longshan culture	4,300–3,800
	Lower Yellow River Plains	Northwestern Henan and southern Hebei	Mid-Late Yangshao culture	5,900–4,500
			Early Longshan culture	4,500–4,300
			Longshan culture	4,300–3,800
		Shandong	Dawenkou culture	5,800–4,400
			Longshan culture	4,400–3,800
	Huai River Plains	Middle Huai River Plains	Mid-Late Yangshao culture	5800–4900
			Houjiazhai culture	6,100–5,500
			Dawenkou culture	5,500–4,300
			Early Longshan culture	4,500–4,300
			Longshan culture	4,300–3,900/3,800
		Lower Huai River Plains	Longqiuzhuang-II culture	6,300–6,000
			Dawenkou culture	5,500–5,100
			Liangzhu culture	5,100–4,300
			Longshan culture	4,300–3,800
	Chengdu Plain		Baodun culture	4,500–3,700
	Three Gorges region		Roughly same as the Jianghan and Dongting Plains	

(cont.)

Region		Culture	Date (cal.BP)
	Jianghan Plains and Dongting Plains	Qujialing-Shijiahe culture	5,200–4,200
		Post-Shijiahe culture	4,200–3,800
	Yangtze Delta region (circum-Taihu Lake region)	Songze culture	6,000–5,300
		Liangzhu culture	5,300–4,300
		Qianshanyang culture	4,400–4,200
		Guangfulin culture	4,200–3,800
	Ningshao Plain	Unclear after Liangzhu	
Coastal regions	Liaodong Bay	Xiaozhushan-II culture	5,500–5,000
		Shantang-I culture	5,000–4,500
		Xiaozhushan-III culture	4,500–4,000
	Jiaodong Peninsula	Dawenkou culture	6,000–4,400
		Longshan culture	4,400–3,800
	Zhejiang coasts	Unclear after Liangzhu	
	Fujian coasts	Tanshishan culture	5,000–4,300
		Huangguashan culture	4,300–3,500
	Guangdong coasts	Guye culture	5,900–5,000
		Hutoupu culture	4,200–3,800

1 Introduction

China's vast geography not only supports one of the longest and most productive agrarian economies of the world, but is also home to a staggering range of biodiversity and domestication of crops and animals of global significance. From Marco Polo (1254–1324) to renowned Ming-and-Qing Dynasties travellers and epigraphic scholars, the vastness and diversity of China's environment had never ceased to inspire vivid imaginations of lives in the imperial cores and peripheries. The intricate relationship between society and the environment continues to define some of the most salient characteristics of historical and contemporary Chinese cultures and societies and has important implications not just for archaeology, but also for understanding China's astonishing recent developments.

More than a century ago, Ferdinand von Richthofen's (1833–1905) detailed descriptions of loess and other environments offered early scientific quests concerning the genesis of the regional environments and how they shaped distinctive local cultures. Environmental studies have since grown exponentially. Parallel to this, archaeology has also undergone an arduous journey and now come to its golden age with an unprecedented boom in funding, research projects, and publications. The data generated through these studies are bewilderingly rich and complex, particularly concerning the *longue durée* of human-environment dynamics (Storozum et al., 2023). Researchers are drawn into research agendas that focus predominantly on the Central Plains and East Plains regions, on agriculture as the main foodway, and on sedentism as the primary lifestyle of ancient societies. Although there is a growing interest in developing alternative perspectives (e.g., Zhang and Hung, 2012), an enormous gap between data, theories, and narratives remains challenging for scholars working in various regions.

Such a methodological and theoretic chasm is particularly acute in the studies of the origins and formation of Chinese Civilisation. What is Chinese Civilisation? When did it begin? And what are its economic and environmental foundations? In the gradual realisation of the multifaceted interactions that contributed to the formation of Chinese Civilisation(s), the importance of environmental diversity has come under close scrutiny. The tasks of this Element are twofold. First, I will marshal new environmental and archaeological data from different regions. Second, with this brief but informative inventory of late-Holocene environmental and archaeological landscapes, I argue that the changing environmental conditions and subsistence adaptations are two of the engines driving increased socio-economic complexity during the late-prehistoric period (from ca. 5,000BP onwards). I will focus on the transitional period between the middle-to-late Holocene (5,000–4,000BP), which coincided with profound environmental and climate changes. It is also the formative period to which the origins of Chinese Civilisation(s) are frequently traced back.

In this Element, I use the plural form of Chinese Civilisations and concentrate on their socio-economic transformations which built on millennia-long developments (Liu and Chen, 2012). These changes spurred great technological innovations, enhanced the ability to modify the environment, and intensified regional interactions, all of which led to the emergence of diverse forms of complex societies and early states in both the 'centres' and 'peripheries', the former often referring to the Central Plains and its immediate vicinities. Such a centre-periphery dichotomy has led to misunderstandings and misinterpretations of archaeological data and will be contested in this Element.

Defining the 'Geographic and Historical' China

The epistemological bounding of late-prehistoric regional civilisations and the formation of 'China' is a long and complicated process. The scope of 'China' covered in this Element roughly coincides with the current political boundaries of the People's Republic of China. It is an environmentally diverse place with three large elevation zones, forming a characteristic three-tiered structure (Figure 1). Landforms in each tier are not flat, but full of variations and slopes, generally declining toward the eastern coasts. A dramatic descent from the

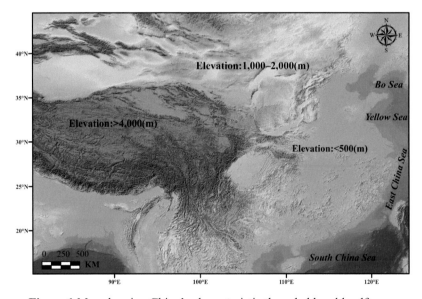

Figure 1 Map showing China's characteristic three-laddered landforms, corresponding to the highlands, lowlands, and coastal regions in this Element.

high-altitude Qinghai-Tibetan Plateau to the Loess Plateau sees an elevation drop from 4,500 m to 3,000–1,000 m. The rolling Loess Plateau then gently transitions to the lowest tier that is dominated by vast alluvial lowlands in the east and south of the country. The Qinghai-Tibetan Plateau is a water tower on the world's third pole, where most of China's major rivers originate. The complicated mechanisms and driving forces that determined Holocene climate on the plateau are being disentangled (Chen F. et al., 2020). Other parts of the country are controlled mainly by the East Asia summer and winter monsoons, and in some parts, the so-called Westerlies (Chen F. et al., 2019). Land, vegetation, and hydrology vary drastically across different terrains and regions.

The long-held perception that China was an isolated place which only began to be widely connected to other parts of the Eurasia since the historical Silk Roads, has been discarded by recent archaeological campaigns (e.g., Flad, 2023; Liu X. et al., 2019). Large-scale and multi-directional connections had been established during the late-prehistoric period, if not earlier, between China and its neighbouring regions and places far afield. The environment has played an instrumental role in fostering and (re)directing these connections. The long and meandering coastlines in Eastern and Southern China encourage seafaring. Some routes of early maritime interactions have been proposed by anthropologists (Chang, 1987; Lin, 1981; Xu, 2019). Archaeological studies have also shed new lights on the north–south and east–west movements of people, things and ideas via numerous islands and land-sea bridges. China's northern border opens to vast steppes that further link to its neighbours in Central Asia, whilst the numerous, large and small mountain and valley corridors in its northwest and southwest also sustain intensive trans-continental interactions. Are there distinctive models for such interactions, such as that proposed by Frachetti (2012) for the 'multiregional' and 'non-uniform' interactions across central Eurasia mobile pastoral groups? Is it true that far-flung connections between the coastal communities were established earlier than those between the inland communities (e.g., Chen and Qu, 2017)? More critically, how do such 'external' processes compare and contrast with the so-called internal environmental coherence (cf. Mo, 2022) that defines the interaction sphere within China?

The interactions between cultures and ethnic groups from different environmental regions, as long proposed by pioneering scholars such as Xiaotong Fei, K.C Chang, and Bingqi Su, were crucial to important technological innovations, cultural adaptations, and socio-economic developments in these regions (Chang, 1989; Su, 1999). Whilst the revelation of this interaction sphere is much celebrated and has significantly pushed forward our understanding of the formation of Chinese Civilisations, subsequent research has focused primarily on the cultural and social factors within this sphere. During the recent academic mania in search of the 'earliest China', many have attempted to provide a holistic narrative on the environmental foundation for the emergence of Chinese Civilisations. However, these narratives often rely predominantly on 'casual' knowledge and are loose on the scientific link between concepts and theories. For instance, it is often speculated that the 'cultural continuum' on the Central Plains benefited from its stable environment (Han, 2015; Song, 2002), but the specific geomorphological, hydrological, pedological conditions that were conducive to agricultural developments and settlement growth are still poorly understood despite some recent efforts (e.g., Lu et al., 2022).

Such a predicament is related to how archaeological research, especially environmental archaeology is organised and carried out in China. A survey of the history of environmental archaeology helps to identify and foster a more robust way to integrate related subjects, through which environmental historians can understand scientific evidence and reasoning whilst science studies scholars value historical-environmental perspectives.

A Short History of Environmental Archaeology in China

A historical-environmental perspective was ingrained in archaeological research in China from its beginning. After almost a century of circuitous development, environmental archaeology in China has emerged as an indispensable field that studies the totality of human–environmental interactions in the past and discerns patterns and trajectories of such dynamic interactions across different time and space.

As a trained geologist, J. G. Andersson (1874–1960) paid great interest to the loess terrains during his excavation at Yangshao 仰韶 in the 1920s in Henan. With Fuli Yuan (1893–1987), a geographer who was trained in the USA, they produced a detailed geomorphic map of the site. Andersson surmised that Yangshao was situated on a flat loess tableland, surrounded by rivers with gentle flow, and the deeply incised gullies (ravines) did not occur until a much later period. Between 1925–1926, Yuan expanded this geomorphological approach in a survey in southern Shanxi before their excavation at the Xiyin 西阴 site. He examined how diverse landforms evolved, focusing on the loess landform, alluvial plains, and river system in the region. His report constituted a large part of the Xinyi-excavation report. Yuan later taught geomorphology at Tsinghua University and Peking University and educated many scholars in environmental archaeology (Storozum et al., 2023).

In 1934, Dinghua Ge (1902–1990) formalised the importance of geology, palaeontology, and climate science in understanding the evolution of past environments and cultures (Ge, 1934). During the excavation at Banpo 半坡

in the 1950s, advances in geology were further integrated with the then-pioneering combination of the Wheeler–Kenyon box grid excavation of a large, open area with detailed stratigraphic recording. The site report formally included palynological and zooarchaeological reports as appendices (IACAS, 1963). The Banpo monograph set a standard format for data presentation for later excavation reports to follow. However, these associated scientific disciplines are often considered supplementary components to archaeological research, which otherwise has an emphasis on material culture. Unlike pioneers like Yuan, some specialists who produce an appendix do not participate in the research planning and excavation. This often results in a simplistic interpretation of the relationship between humans and their environment, hindering cross-regional comparisons.

As early as the 1950s, Siyong Liang (1904–1954) examined geomorphological evidence from over 70 'Longshan 龙山-period' sites and suggested that most sites were situated on gentle tablelands ideal for water usage and flood prevention (Liang, 1954). In the 1990s, several influential environmental archaeological projects conducted on the Central Plains further established a holistic, long-term perspective of cultural adaptations to the environment. One such project, the *Origin of Chinese Civilisation*, aimed to reveal the timing, processes, and mechanisms of the Chinese civilisation's formation. The environmental archaeology component of it focused on characteristics of landscapes and environments on the Central Plains in its initial phase but quickly expanded to many other regions such as the Lower Yellow River, the Yangtze Valleys, and the West Liao River. Following this state-level initiative, more geomorphological and geoarchaeological surveys applied different analytical methods at both key archaeological sites and their surrounding environments, yielding fruitful results (DSDST and DMSCR, 2009). This renaissance of the early tradition established by Yuan, Liang, and others emphasised the crucial role of geomorphological environment and hydrology in fostering long-term settlement developments and the so-called 'cultural continuum' in ancient China (see below).

Many systematic regional surveys have been carried out since 1990s by specialists in archaeobotany, geoarchaeology, GIS-spatial analysis, and other related subjects from international collaborative teams, adopting a truly regional perspective. A survey in the middle eastern Luoyang Basin of the Yi-Luo 伊洛 River valley on the Central Plains illustrated the relationship between prehistoric settlements and the environment that was instrumental to the rise of early complex societies in the region. Geoarchaeologists in the team provided a wealth of detailed, on-the-ground information about soil composition, land characteristics, and natural resources (IACASS & CAUJATYRB, 2019). This new line of inquiry allows archaeologists and geoarchaeologists to avoid oversimplification in their broad-scale characterisation of the palaeo-environment, and to evaluate how people in the past directly engaged with key natural resources for settlement building, farming, animal husbandry, craft production, and other economic activities.

In synthesising recent environmental and archaeological data, this Element builds on some of the themes from previous studies on landform and settlement distribution, and natural resources and subsistence strategies, whilst also extending its focus to connectivity and movement, and landscape modification and adaptability. It employs a multi-layered investigative approach that interrogates both macro-scale narratives on landform and environmental changes and micro-level evidence on land use and economic activities (e.g., rice cultivation in early rice fields). It advocates for a geoarchaeological perspective that seeks to establish more robust understanding of multi-levelled interactions between societies and their environments.

Only through these analyses can we truly appreciate models of human adaptations to the environment and trajectories to the rise of Chinese Civilisations. These models adopt a comparative regional perspective, ranging from the so-called Northern model that suggests that climate and environment in Northern China did not support large-scale, affluent agriculture and hence restrict the growth of highly stratified society (Han, 2003), to the Central Plains model and the Eastern model. The latter two advocate a 'cultural continuum' in the Central Plains from the environmental perspective (Han, 2017; He et al., 2022; Lu et al., 2022) and an opulent and mortuary tradition with pronounced social stratification in the Dawenkou and Liangzhu cultures (Han, 2003), respectively. These models touch upon important issues such as cultural continuity and socio-economic transformations in different regions and thus serve as a useful starting point to comprehend China's environmental and cultural diversity and its deep prehistoric origins.

Whilst recent scholarship has begun to acknowledge the complex interplay between natural and cultural processes that contributed to the formation of these zones, defining their spatial and temporal boundaries remains challenging, particularly since some of these boundaries inevitably extend beyond the modern borders of nation states. This Element divides the environment of late-prehistoric China into highlands, lowlands, and coastal areas (see Li, 2021 for discussion on Longshan-period highlands). The highlands refer to most of the first- and second-tiered land, whilst the lowlands include vast low-lying plains on the third tier. The latter also contains the coastal areas. There are regions such as the Chengdu Basin, which are situated between the highlands and lowlands and serve as key communication nodes between them. Additionally, the lowland-and-highland distinction also exists within these regions (e.g., the circum-Songshan Mountain region). The geographic boundary in such cases might seem quite arbitrary. Therefore, this

Element's definitions of highlands, lowlands, and coastal areas are intentionally broad and accommodating, including those transitional zones that have often been overlooked. One of the benefits of adopting such a geographic division is that it avoids the conventional centre-periphery dichotomy which, as stated briefly above, seems obsolete in a radically changing research landscape in China where large amount of data have been collected from multiple regions (cf. Flad and Chen, 2013). I seek to characterise some of the key environmental processes between 5,000–4,000BP in different regions and understand how these processes paved the way for the remarkable socio-economic adaptations, resilience, and reorganisations that eventually led to the rise of early states and complex societies in late-prehistoric China.

2 The Monsoons, the Dust, and the Water

Monsoons, tectonics, and sea level changes are the three main forces that create China's diverse climates and environments. Tectonic events are the earth-shattering forces directly creating some of the dramatic landforms across China, including its characteristic mountains, gorges, and basins. The elevation of the Qinghai-Tibetan Plateau resulting from continuing tectonic uplift from the collision of the Indian and Asian Plates (Ding et al., 2022) forever separates northwest China's climates and environments from those of other parts of East Asia and South Asia. But relatively speaking, neotectonic activities operate on a much larger timescale and thus have less evident impact on the Holocene environment, although there is increasing archaeological evidence of devastation caused by earthquakes in different regions of prehistoric China (see Hu et al., 2023 for prehistoric earthquake in the Central Plains ca. 5,000BP and Section 3 for the example at Lajia). In contrast, the monsoon systems, which originated at least 40 ma ago (Tardif et al., 2020), have a more subtle yet more enduring effect on the climate and environment. Sea-level fluctuation interacts with climate and tectonic changes and significant impacts landform and hydrology along the coastal regions.

When the Wind Blows, All Other Factors Are Small

'Holocene' is a geological term referring to the warm epoch in which we are living. The Holocene climate systems in East Asia, including the East Asian monsoon, the Indian monsoon, and the so-called Westerlies (Figure 2), are independent of and interact with each other. Although these systems are linked in undiscovered manners, minute changes in one system can lead to different monsoonal conditions in other systems. When the East Asian Summer Monsoons (EASM) and Indian Summer Monsoons (ISM) prevail, the moist monsoon fronts bring abundant rainfall in the summer, whilst the climate is dominated by northern cool air with

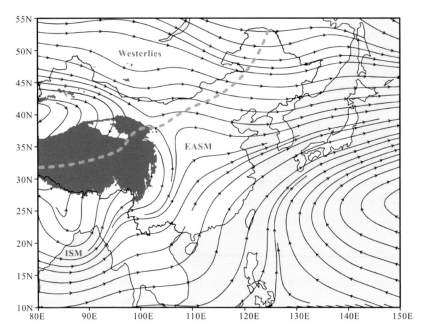

Figure 2 The three main climate systems in China and East Asia, the
EASM, ISM, and Westerlies systems; grey area referring to areas > 3,000 masl.
Modified after Chen et al. (2015a).

meagre precipitation in the winter, resulting in a typical Asian monsoon climate
with a warm and wet summer and a cold and dry winter. Holocene EASM and ISM
display temporal and spatial variations due to changing monsoon intensity. The
EASM moves northward to as far north as ca. 40°N and the intensity of the rainfall
belts decreases. On a temporal basis, Holocene climate experienced a classical
three-staged development: a warming early Holocene (12,000–9,000BP) with
steadily improved moisture and temperature, a so-called Holocene Climatic
Optimum (HCO, 9,000–6,000BP) when humidity and rainfall reached the climax,
and a return to drier and cooler conditions during the late Holocene (from ca.
5,000BP) with intensified seasonality. These broad-scale changes are, however,
underlined by short-term and small-scale fluctuations.

The HCO is considered 'the postglacial interval of most equable climate,
with warm temperatures and abundant rainfall' (An et al., 2000: 744). Despite
persisting scholarly disagreements on its onset and duration, more high-
resolution (i.e., on centennial scale) environmental records have allowed
scholars to disentangle the possible time-transgressive nature of the HCO
(Zhang J. et al., 2011; Zhang Z. et al., 2021). Broadly speaking, in northern
and northeast monsoonal China, maximum precipitation occurred as early as ca.

9,000BP, whilst the monsoonal southern region experienced a later onset of the HCO during the early-to-middle Holocene, and some regions in South and Southeast China entered the HCO as late as 3,000BP (An et al., 2000; Wang et al., 2010). The transition to the HCO marked an increased climate stability in these regions, with less decadal or centennial rainfall fluctuations (Zhang Z. et al., 2021). Such climate stability would have been instrumental to the succession and growth of prehistoric societies with established agricultural economies particularly in millet-growing areas that are prone to drought.

The boundaries between the monsoonal zones are fluid, especially in regions where the EASM, ISM, and Westerlies meet as illustrated in Figure 2. The eastern plains and coastal areas, the Tibetan Plateau, and the steppes and northwest region are dominated by the EASM, ISM, and Westerlies, respectively. Much of China's second tier coincides with the monsoonal boundaries and is influenced by multiple climate systems. The latter created some complex climate events, especially in the arid and semi-arid zones, during the transition from the middle-to-late Holocene. Stalagmite isotope records from caves have shown that the gradual but prolonged aridification process began as early as 5,000BP and lasted for several millennia. Wang et al.'s (2005) five-year-resolution oxygen isotope record from the Dongge 董哥 cave in Southern China identifies a steadily declining curve of monsoon intensity that is punctuated by eight 'weak monsoon events' including the 8.2 and 4.2 kaBP events. Comparatively, records from the Sanbao 三宝 cave in Central China point to a decline of monsoon intensity from 6,500BP onwards (Dong et al., 2010). Whilst there is a need to reconcile these different stalagmite records and compare them with other data such as lacustrine sediments (e.g., Chen et al., 2015a), a shared pattern of Holocene moisture change can be gauged from the available records (Liu Z. et al., 2014). Such changes might be described as a spiral decrement, characterised by increased decadal fluctuations in precipitation (Jiang et al., 2013; Wang et al., 2005) (Figure 3a). The oscillations around some late-Holocene climate events (e.g., the 4.2 kaBP event) are particularly evident. Modern meteorological records in some Asian monsoon regions also show extreme variations in annual precipitation, oscillating between 260 and 1,200 mm (Li et al., 2023).

Another challenge facing climatologists is the Westerlies system, prevalent in Northwest China and other regions in Central Asia. Climatologists have observed a recent shift from a 'warm-dry to a warm-humid climate' due to global warming in the region (Chen et al., 2008). Some even postulate a cold-wet and warm-dry climatic association that is opposite to the typical warm-wet and cold-dry monsoonal climate. Chen F. et al.'s (2019) synthesis illustrates these out-of-phase climatic behaviours (Figure 3b). Precipitation in Northwest

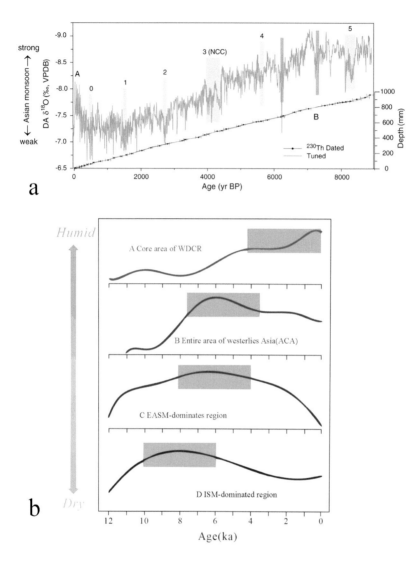

Figure 3 (a): Fluctuating frequencies and amplitudes of stalagmite oxygen isotope values from the Dongge cave caused by Holocene climate change; yellow bars show timing of climate events. Redrawn after Wang et al. (2005). (b): Anti-phasing climate change in the Westerlies area compared to other climate regions, redrawn after Chen et al. (2019).

China increased during the transition from the middle-to-late Holocene, with 'the most humid period occurring during the late Holocene', in clear contrast to other monsoonal regions. This also impacts the aforementioned 'transitional zones' between the Westerlies and monsoonal systems which enjoyed a relatively more humid climate and more favourable ecological condition between 5,000–4,000BP (Chen F. et al., 2019). The lake level in the Daihai region in current Inner Mongolia, for instance, remained high and the local soil was developed with good vegetative cover (Xiao et al., 2004). Similar evidence can be seen in other neighbouring regions (Feng et al., 2006).

The 4.2 kaBP event marked an abrupt return to dry and cold conditions around 4,200BP, causing abnormal rainfall and increased floods and droughts. It is widely considered as a catalyst for major socio-political changes across Northern-Hemisphere societies (Weiss, 2017, 2022). However, its impact on Holocene climate and societies in China and other parts of East Asia is less clear, partly because of the complex climate systems just described, but also due to the complicated feedback mechanisms between climate and the society, which necessitates greater research effort to disentangle, and we are not yet in a position to establish a clear link between this event and some profound socio-political changes in the region (but see He et al., 2022; Jaffe and Hein, 2021).

When the Dust Settles, the Rolling Terrains Become Flat

The aeolian activities that mantle thick loess deposits on the East Asia continent couple closely with rhythm and tempo of the monsoonal climate changes. These activities exhibit phenomenal scale, duration, and magnitude, and their intensity synchronises with the glacial and interglacial cycles, resonating roughly with the Marine Isotope Stages and Ice Core records (Kohfeld et al., 2006; Porter, 2001). During the Pleistocene glacial periods, strong wintery winds brought abundant dust from deserts in Siberia, Mongolia, and Northern and Northwest China, blanketing the vast territory of North China and turning rugged pre-Pleistocene terrains into flat and mostly homogeneous loess landscapes. The loess region covers ca. 638,000 km^2 and stretches much further south than conventionally understood, including south of the middle and lower Yangtze River valleys (Figure 4a). At the heartland of the Loess Plateau is the enormity of loess deposition, reaching more than 200 m in thickness in some places. A typical loess sequence consists of the Lishi, Wuchang, and Malan loess, corresponding to the early-, middle-, and late-Pleistocene glacial periods, respectively, and the Holocene loess.

Loess is a key resource for societal developments in both historical and modern times. Its loose structure and homogeneous texture result in a distinctive vertical cleavage. These properties are considered engineering advantages that promote the durability and stability of loess architecture. The cave houses invented in the late-Neolithic period continue to be used and, in many cases, are favoured by modern residents. These houses are dug deeply and

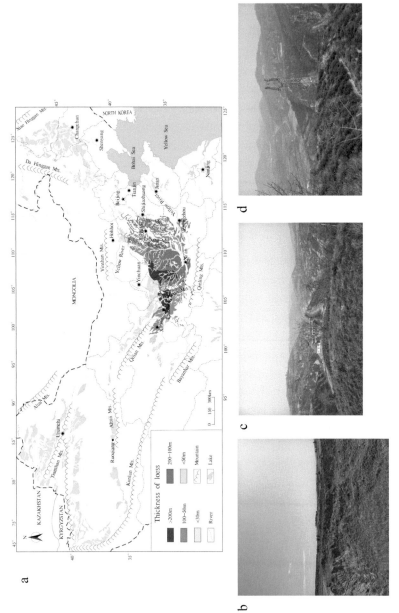

Figure 4 (a): Distribution of loess in China, modified after Li et al. (2020). (b): *Yuan* loess tableland in Datong City, Shanxi Province. (c–d): *Liang* and *mao* loess tablelands in Shaanxi Province.

horizontally into the loess cliff, benefiting from the vertical-cleavage structure and representing one of the greatest architectural innovations in the loess region (see Section 3).

Loess and loessic palaeosol's rich nutrients and porous structure are conducive to agricultural production. Loess contains nutrients in various forms, including Ca, Si, Al, K, and many other elements (Liu, 1985: 360). Some have vividly compared the loess-laden winds to a 'sky river' which replenishes loess farmlands in a way similar to the annual floods of the Nile River in Egypt (Liu, 2003). Despite being a relatively 'quieter' epoch, the Holocene period, especially during those dry spells, still experiences frequent dust storms, which can be unpleasant and destructive. But they also bring nutritious sediments for agricultural production. The top (A) horizon of the middle-to-late-Holocene soil is exceptionally thick and contains abundant newly added sediments, mainly from the wind-blown loess. These properties were valuable, especially in prehistoric and historical times before the advent of deep ploughing and large-scale use of fertiliser. In *Classic of Poetry*, ancestors of the Zhou people eulogised that 'the plain (loess tableland) of Zhouyuan 周原, spreading out to the south, was so fertile and fair that sweet in the mouth, were its bitterest herbs' (translation by Allen, 1891)

But life on the loess land presents numerous challenges too. Among them are erosion, drought, and their profound ecological consequences. Erosion occurs when rainwater hits the dry, vegetation-depleted surface. Because of the loose and porous structure of loess, once it starts, surface erosion accelerates as land use and other forms of disturbance intensify. Erosion process is responsible for creating the *yuan* 塬, *liang* 梁, and *mao* 峁 landforms in the loess region (Figure 4b–d). Initially, erosion incises vast and flat loess land into large-sized *yuan* tablelands, which are then cut into smaller *liang* tablelands through gully erosion. As erosion intensifies, the sloped surface *liang* tablelands is incised into isolated *mao* loess hills. Many of the erosion gullies on the loess land are up to several hundred metres deep and several dozen kilometres long. Although it is difficult to determine the exact date when severe erosion began, excavation and survey evidence suggests that some large erosion gullies already existed during the late Holocene. Therefore, erosion must have already been a problem that residents of large late-prehistoric sites, such as the Taosi 陶寺 site, had to face.

When the Water Prevails, Lakes and Rivers Swell Up

Although loess accumulates continuously or semi-continuously, its geomorphological effects are rarely noticeable on a short-term basis. In contrast, the rivers and their incessant, sometimes raging water, are powerful forces that erode, transport, and deposit weathered materials over long distance. China has more than 50,000 rivers, although many of them are disappearing (Toor, 2013). Among them are some of the world's largest and longest rivers, such as the Yellow and Yangtze Rivers, and their famous tributaries, with awe-inspiring abilities to create and transform the land. Some of China's most iconic landscapes, such as the North China Plain, are the products of these extraordinary processes. These channels transport abundant water and eroded sediments from highlands on China's first tier to lowlands on its second and third tiers, creating numerous lakes, wetlands, and plains. This section sketches out broad-scale hydrological and sedimentation characteristics and fluvial morphologies of the Yellow and Yangtze Rivers.

After overcoming the obstacle of the deep Sanmenxia 三门峡 Gorge, the Yellow River began its remarkable land-forming journey eastward, creating vast plains and alluvial fans. It is estimated that the Yellow River carried around 8×10^{12} tons of sediments during the Holocene, with a particularly high annual sediment load in the past 2,500 years due to severe erosion in the upper and middle reaches (Peng et al., 2010; Wang et al., 2016). However, due to the heavily silt-laden water, the rivers are prone to channel silting, migration, and avulsion, resulting in devastating consequences (Figure 5). The frequency and magnitude

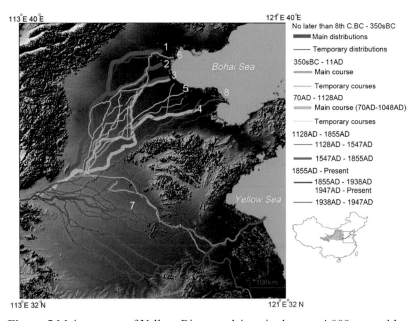

Figure 5 Major events of Yellow-River avulsions in the past 4,000 years; blue shade in lower right shows the distribution of loess, after Chen Y. et al. (2012).

of the Lower Yellow River channel avulsion increased evidently in the past 2,500 years, indicating a positive correlation between channel behaviours and human activities (Yu et al., 2020).

It might be difficult to perceive that North China, given its current semi-arid condition, was once home to numerous lakes and wetlands, but the warm and humid middle-Holocene era saw their proliferation as confirmed by historical accounts and palaeo-environmental evidence. Lakes and wetlands were present not only in alluvial lowlands but also in higher-elevation areas such as loess hills (Lu et al., 2021). The spatial and temporal fluctuations of these waterbodies have significant ramifications for understanding prehistoric settlement patterns in the region (Sections 3 and 4).

The Yangtze River originates from the Tibetan Plateau and joins with numerous tributaries as it navigates through challenging terrains, including the famous Three Gorges, before flowing into its middle section and giving rise to several massive alluvial plains, including the Liyang 澧阳, Dongting 洞庭, Jianghan 江汉, and Poyang 鄱阳 Lake plains (Figure 6). Late Pleistocene and Holocene alluvial and lacustrine sediments lie atop middle-Pleistocene red clay and/or loess in these plains. On the piedmonts are alluvial sediments, forming the so-called high-alluvial plains (30–40 masl), whilst the middle parts are typically characterised

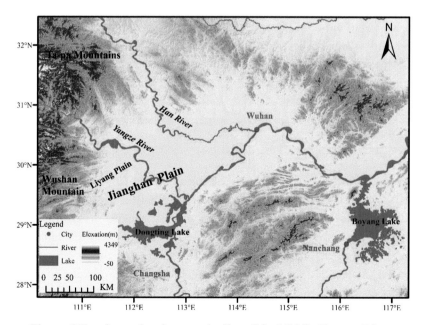

Figure 6 Terrains and major waterbodies of the Middle Yangtze River, including the Liyang, Jianghan, and Dongting plains.

by thick alluvial and lacustrine sediments, forming low-lying plains (<30 masl) (Guo et al., 2016; Mo, 2020). Remnant loess hills (with 1–2 m relative height) and high mountains (>200 masl) are scattered between these alluvial lowlands. The rising water from the terminal Pleistocene to the early Holocene brought in abundant weathered sediments, quickly filling up incised gullies, and eventually creating many lakes which were frequently flooded (Zhao and Mo, 2020). In the Liyang Plain, for instance, the early-Holocene landscape comprised alluvial lowlands, crisscrossed by rivers and many small lakes, with scattered hills occupied by early-Holocene settlements (Guo et al., 2016). Regional hydrology stabilised from 7,000BP onwards, and between 5,500–5,000BP, the regional water level started to drop, with more frequent fluctuations in lake hydrology and the emergence of more land (Zhao and Mo, 2020). The implications of such hydrological and geomorphological processes to prehistoric occupation are discussed in Section 4.

The Lower Yangtze River underwent similar geomorphological and hydrological changes during the Holocene. The early-Holocene sea-level rise led to a high water table and continuous alluvial aggradation that gradually filled up the late-Pleistocene loess landscape which was similarly characterised by incised valleys and undulating terrains (Wang et al., 2018a). Despite the challenges posed by water, the Majiabang 马家浜 people (7,000–6,300BP) and their contemporaries inhabited the newly emerged land and remnant hills. Over the following millennia, both vertical and lateral aggradation dominated land accretion as high water table brought in abundant sediments and also caused frequent overbank flows that impacted the land-forming processes across and beyond the alluvial lowlands (Zhao et al., 2022). The phenomenal rise of the Songze 崧泽 (6,000–5,300BP) and Liangzhu 良渚 (5,300–4,300BP) cultures marked a region-wide adaptation to these environmental processes (Section 4).

When the Sea Level Fluctuates, High Tides Push Far Inland

The one- to two-degree temperature rise caused by the HCO is substantial, but its impact on the environment might not be immediately evident. In contrast, the magnitude of sea-level rise is significantly greater, resulting in submersion of expansive coastal and inland areas. In most coastal regions of China, the Holocene sea level experienced a steep rising curve of almost 40 m from 15,000BP to 8,000BP, followed by a steady but much slower rising rate until it reached a middle-Holocene highstand between 7,000–6,000BP. The sea level then remained close to the present level with some small-magnitude oscillations during the middle-to-late Holocene (Figure 7). Zong (2004) compares tectonic, subsidence, and other local factors from six east and south coastal regions in

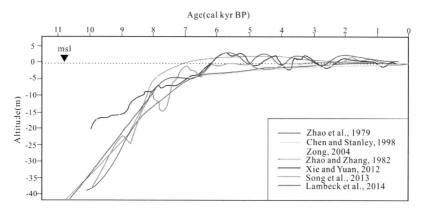

Figure 7 Simulated curves showing Holocene sea-level change in Eastern China, modified after Zhao et al. (2022).

China and found that the high middle-Holocene sea level tends to occur earlier (by almost 1,000 years) in larger deltas than smaller ones. In Fujian and Guangdong, for instance, a middle-Holocene highstand, of an extra 1–2 m height, might have occurred due to crustal movements (Wang L. et al., 2022).

The formation of the Yellow River delta and its surrounding regions began with a marine transgression around 9,000BP. From 7,000–6,000BP, seawater inundation reached the westernmost part of the Bohai Bay, forming discontinuous chenier ridges that accelerated deltaic deposition towards the seafront. However, due to its highly mobile and intertwining river channels, the delta evolved into a super lobe structure with alluvial sediments and abandoned river channels superimposing on top of one another. At least nine to ten of these lobes were formed during the Holocene and the annual sediment loads that contributed to their formation saw a steady increase since historical times (Hu et al., 2021). Combined with oscillating seawater, these lobe structures create some of the most complex groundwater and ecosystems, which are attractive to humans but challenging to control.

In the Yangtze River mouth, delta deposition began around 8,000BP with the maximum flood surface moving >100 km seaward. This was followed by several sedimentation hiatuses and landward retreat of shelf sediments after 6,000BP. The river mouth developed into a funnel shape, with a tidal inlet in the upper valley and a ridge offshore. A proper delta gradually took shape in the river mouth front in the late Holocene, when human-induced sedimentation also increased (Wang et al., 2018a). Further south from the delta are the Hangzhou Bay, which was separated from the palaeo-Yangtze valley in the early Holocene (Zhang et al., 2015), and the Ningshao 宁绍 Plain in its southeast. During the early Holocene, the palaeo-Yaojiang 姚江 valley and Ningbo Bay experienced rapid siltation with abundant marine sediment through tidal activities, including the 'downdrift' from the Yangtze River mouth. However, the water regime remained volatile with prevalent seawater condition. Sedimentation rate in the muddy coasts of the region slowed down from 7,000BP onwards, gradually transitioning to coastal marshes and floodplains (Lyu et al., 2021). Despite the persisting hydrological volatility and environmental vulnerability, intensive archaeological investigations have shown an early and developed sedentary culture on the Ningshao Plain, many of which were sheltered by coastal embayments.

Sea-level change and its impact on the formation of deltaic and coastal landforms and environments are closely tied to prehistoric human occupation. Once sea level gradually receded and hydrology became more stable, people moved to deltaic and estuary landscapes for agriculture and other purposes. Late-prehistoric colonisation of these places created flourishing civilisations.

Developing the Themes

The major natural forces that shape China's diverse environments across high-lands and lowlands provide only part of the picture. The increasingly larger-scale infrastructure constructions in these places and landscape modifications by late-prehistoric societies had started to exert some impact on the environment, the legacy of which we continue to live with today (Chen S. et al., 2020; Zhang S. et al., 2020). There is an increasingly reductive and even depreciatory altitude towards the ecological viability of China's 'resource-intensive growth' (Lander, 2021: 13). This is largely because of our reflexive reaction to the powerful environmentalist movement in the context of China's rapid industrialisation and enormous urban development, but it also stems from an understanding of China's deep and complicated environmental past. There is also, however, a danger in either romanticising or stigmatising the environmental past without considering human's position in these processes. The human–environment relationship is far from straightforward, as advocates of the early Anthropocene suggest (cf. Hundson, 2014), and is full of progressive, regressive, and transgressive altitudes towards modifying landscape, expanding territory, and adapting to new conditions.

Environmental archaeology promotes a close marriage between historical accounts and environmental records of past ecological conditions. It has helped us to outline the silhouettes of diverse ecosystems in different regions of China and understand how these might have affected human adaptations and cultural resilience. As we investigate the distinctive environments and lifestyles in late-prehistoric China, we will bring together archaeological data not only from the well-studied Yellow and Yangtze River valleys but also from equally important but often overlooked regions such as the Huai 淮 River. We will compare and contrast these diverse late-prehistoric lifeways and evaluate their profound legacies, some of which are forgotten, whilst others are inherited. We will also tell the stories of lowland and coastal societies of farmers, hunters-gatherers, and seafarers who benefited tremendously from the improved geomorphological and hydrological conditions during the middle-to-late Holocene, and explore if their growth, expansion, and transformation sheds new light on some of the environmental problems facing contemporary society.

3 The Highlands

The term 'highlands' here refers to the high-altitude plains, basins and plateaus on China's first and second tiers, including the Mongolia Plateau, Loess Plateau, and the Yungui Plateau (this region will not be discussed due to data scarcity). These regions have recently become focus of environmental, archaeological, and historical research as they were crucibles of technological innovation, inter-regional migration, and significant social development in the past. The independent geographic zones and the intermediate land surrounding them, such as the Chengdu Basin, Fen-Wei 汾渭 Basin, and the West Liao 辽 River, provided shelters for prehistoric groups facing escalating climatic uncertainties and growing competition for land and other resources, and hence fostered great socio-economic developments during the late Holocene. The environment, ecology, settlements, and subsistence strategies of these regions are summarised below.

The Qinghai-Tibetan Plateau: Migrant Farmers and Herders Peopling the Roof of the World

Recent archaeological and environmental studies have uncovered remarkable stories of human adaptation and colonisation to the harsh and challenging environment on the Qinghai-Tibetan Plateau (Figure 8a). In particular, the late Holocene witnessed a consolidation and expansion of permanent human occupation on the plateau. One of the challenges to live on the plateau is high altitude (>4,000 msl) with harsh climates, causing hypoxia in humans and other lives. Temperature and precipitation in the plateau fluctuate according to topographic gradients, which slope broadly from northwest to southeast (from >5,000 m to ca. 3,000 masl), resulting in dramatic ecological transformations. Few trees and only some shrubs and grasses grow above 3,000 masl. In the east and southeast Tibetan Plateau, however, there are many low-altitude river valley systems where lush vegetation thrives (d'Alpoim-Guedes and Aldenderfer, 2020). Central Tibet is also dotted with some lower-altitude valleys, whilst western Tibet has far fewer.

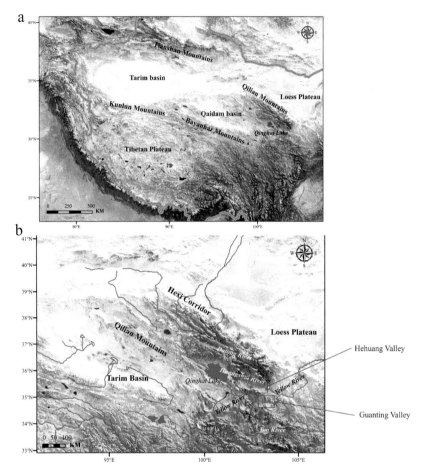

Figure 8 Landforms on and around the Qinghai-Tibetan Plateau (a) and Hexi Corridor (b).

During the early-to-middle Holocene, climate on the plateau was warm, due to high summer insolation caused by a strong ISM. The mean annual temperature during the late Holocene remains hard to reconstruct (Zhao et al., 2017). Recent syntheses show an emerging pattern of divergent moisture conditions between the northern and southern parts of the plateau as reflected in lake-level changes (Chen F. et al., 2020). The plateau has numerous freshwater and saltwater lakes, covering a total area of 520 km^2. Many lakes remain unfrozen even during winter, despite the high altitude, and serve not only as critical sources of water but also as sanctuaries for animals and humans. In particular, lakes that enjoyed a high lake level during the middle-to-late Holocene were attractive places to early human settlements.

Recent archaeological campaigns have made significant progress in understanding what, when, where, and how different crops and animals made their way to the plateau in association with humans. Cultivars including wheat, barley, naked barley, pigs, sheep, and goats arrived on the plateau at different times and through different mechanisms. Some gradually became intrinsic parts of the plateau life, whilst others vanished without leaving many traces. However, before the arrival of farmer immigrants with their cultivars, indigenous hunting-and-gathering groups already existed and were exploring a wide range of wild plants and animals (d'Alpoim-Guedes and Aldenderfer, 2020). Even with established farming settlements, their diets still contained foraged food, painting a complicated picture of the early encounters between farmer and foragers.

Among the highest altitude archaeological sites where domesticated cultivars are present is the Mabu Co 玛不错 site, situated by a lake some 4,400 masl. The site's wealth of cultural remains as well as faunal and floral assemblages have spurred scientific inquiries into the modes in which humans established this high-altitude settlement ca. 4,000BP. However, the domesticated millets found here were unlikely to have been cultivated locally but rather obtained from regional trade (Xiaoyan Yang, personal communication). A breakthrough in prehistoric plateau agriculture occurred ca. 3,500BP when evidence of cultivation of naked barley, wheat, oat, rye, and foxtail millet is found at sites such as Changguogou 昌果沟 at 3,600 masl (Chen et al., 2015b). The warmer climate between 5,000–4,200BP might have enabled millets to be cultivated in areas just below 3,000 msl, as evidenced by findings from Zongri 宗日, Karuo 卡若, and several other sites (d'Alpoim-Guedes et al., 2016). Residents of these sites built many houses and cemeteries, with increasingly sophisticated craft industries (Huo, 2010; Luo, 2015), but the investment in hydrology and soil to grow crops seemed to be minimal, and the establishment of agriculture likely took several millennia to complete.

As frontier farmers and herders moved gradually upwards, especially when their expansion to high-altitude places coincided with some cold episodes, the 'cold-hardy barley' and sheep were vital to the establishment of farms above 4,000 masl (Chen et al., 2015b). Many discoveries have illustrated that millets arrived in northeastern Tibet from Central China before appearing in central Tibet (Chen et al., 2015b), whilst wheat and barley might have come from multiple routes. Given the early occurrence of wheat and barley around the borders of the plateau, it is reasonable to suggest that they were introduced from the northeastern margins via the 'Inner Asian mountain corridor' during the fourth millennium BP (d'Alpoim-Guedes and Aldenderfer, 2020). Additionally, the southern and western Himalayas might be another region for the spread of such exotic crops (Gao et al., 2021).

Domesticated pigs occurred at several >3,000 msl sites (e.g., Karuo and Xiao'enda 小恩达) in southeastern Tibet between 5,000–4,000BP, having arrived from the Upper Yellow River (Wang et al., 2023). Living almost at the altitudinal limit for pig raising (and millet cultivation), the Karuo people also relied on hunting and gathering to sustain their sedentary life. The importance of pigs declined whilst domesticated sheep and cattle became more important in the following millennium, likely due to their higher tolerance to colder and drier conditions. The incorporation between these cultivars, farmers, and herders followed different trajectories and enabled diverse adaptations to high-altitude environments (>3,500 masl). One of the most remarkable achievements made by these pioneering populations was the adoption of an agropastoral system, in which herded animals and cultivated crops tolerated and thrived in high-altitude environments. Some cultivated crops might have been consumed by both humans and animals (Gao et al., 2021; Song et al., 2021). Other cultivars, such as buckwheat and yak, were also important in this distinctive agropastoral economy, but their histories are more elusive to untangle.

As an alternative to the model focusing on the conquest of high-altitude places, some have proposed an agricultural thermal niches model to understand the establishment and spread of prehistoric agriculture in the plateau, emphasising the low-elevation river valleys. They suggest that 'Tibetan farmers in the past, as today, practiced agriculture in the deeply cut lower-altitude river valleys on the Tibetan Plateau, leaving large parts of the plateau as potential refugia for hunter-gatherers' (d'Alpoim-Guedes et al., 2016: 517). Regardless of the debate, low-altitude valley bottoms and other geographic units such as lakeside terraces would have been important habitats through which people, animals, and plants could move sustainably in their journey towards to the world's roof.

The Hexi Corridor and the He-Huang Valleys: Frontier Farmers and Herders Taking Root

The Hexi 河西 Corridor and the He-Huang 河湟 Valleys in the Upper Yellow River (Figure 8b) are a crucial link between the Loess Plateau and the Qinghai-Tibetan Plateau, as well as Central and even Western Asia, and cradle of important innovations which bring closer the agricultural zones on the Central Plains and the agropastoral zones on the plateaus. The region's average elevation is around 1,600 masl and its arid climate has an annual temperature of 5–9 °C and annual precipitation between 500 and 400 mm. The Holocene climate saw a steady decrease of mean annual temperature from 11.8 °C around 7,000BP to 9.5 °C around 3,800BP, with small-magnitude fluctuations thereafter. There was also an evident reduction in mean annual precipitation by ca. 170 mm, although 4,300–3,900BP might be a comparatively wetter period (Ji et al., 2005; Zhao et al., 2018).

The vast space between the Yellow River and Huang River valleys is dotted by a string of gorges and basins. The Guanting 官厅 Basin is one of them (Figure 8b). It sits between the Jishi 积石 Gorge and Sigou 寺沟 Gorge, covering an area of ca. 53 km². Landforms on the two flanks of the river are dominated by hilly terrains and multi-ordered river terraces, which are constantly altered by surface erosion process. The second and third-ordered terraces are ca. 30–40 m and 90–100 m higher than the current river water level, respectively. Sandwiched between the terraces in the western end of the basin are alluvial fans and tablelands. The terrace surfaces contain late-Pleistocene and early-Holocene loess and paleosols, upon which many late-Holocene sites have been discovered. Lanzhou basin is another riverine basin with typical loess land and terraces that are distributed roughly northwest-southeast in a faulted plate. The middle-to-late Holocene environment was relatively mild and conducive to growth of prehistoric settlements. However, despite its better condition for farming than that of the Qinghai-Tibetan Plateau, land is fragmentary and water is hard to obtain, both significantly restricting agricultural growth before irrigation became available.

The middle-to-late Holocene He-Huang Valleys saw a surge in prehistoric population. The Majiayao 马家窑 culture period (5,300–4,500BP) marked the beginning of settlement congregation, and by the Machang 马厂 phase (4,300–4,000BP), the settlements were concentrated in the lower Huang River basin and next to the Yellow River lowlands as more settlements moved from higher to lower altitudes, representative of a shift of regional focus toward the east (Jiang et al., 2020) (Figure 9). Many settlements also dwelt on the terrace tops with gentle gradients, which provided the most desirable environment for the growing farming society. Settlement density declined in the following Qijia 齐家 culture period (4,200–3,600BP), prompting some to move to lowlands nearer the Yellow River before settlements congregated again in roughly the same places in the subsequent Kayue 卡约 and Xindian 辛店 culture period (3,600–2,700BP) (Dong et al., 2013; Niu, 2018; Qiu et al., 2019). The ebb and flow of prehistoric settlements resulted in changes in subsistence strategies in the region. The concentration of Majiayao settlements towards the lower-altitude places closer to river might be a deliberate choice for more arable land, whilst the venture into the higher-altitude locations indicated the importance of agropastoral economy during the Bronze Age. Kayue culture sites are mostly distributed in high-altitude places, practising sheep herding. Conversely, the contemporary farming settlements of the Xindian culture were concentrated in the low-elevation basin (Dong et al., 2013).

The region's prosperous late-prehistoric cultures were shattered by earthquakes and associated natural disasters. The most explicit example of prehistoric earthquakes comes from the Qijia-culture site of Lajia 喇家 where fissures

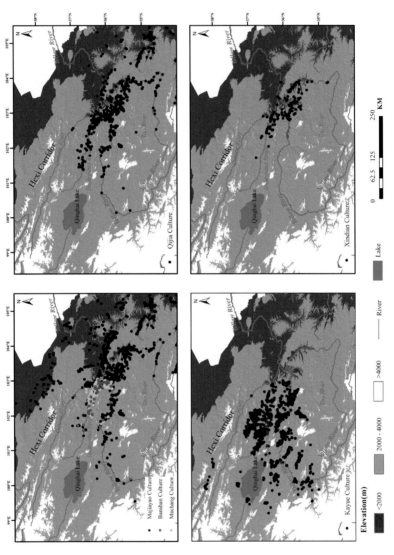

Figure 9 Distributions of prehistoric sites in and around the Hexi Corridor region, site data from NCHA (1996, 2011).

caused by the earthquakes are commonly seen in houses and surrounding the site (Huang et al., 2013). Conglomerated red clay sediments deposited during landslips and landslides provide evidence of catastrophic floods and mudflows that buried the site. Excavation reveals a chilling scene of the devastation brought to the prehistoric occupants by these natural disasters that took place between ca. 3,900–3,800BP. Many human skeletons were found in different postures on the living floors, covered by the conglomerated red clay (Huang et al., 2013). Interestingly, whilst houses situated on higher-elevation places (1,790–1,795 masl) were destroyed and covered by the mudflows and land-slides, the burial of those on relatively lower-altitude places (1,788–1,790 masl) seemed not to be affected by these catastrophic geological events. Popular narratives suggest that a landslide-damming lake formed due to the blockage of the gorge after the earthquake caused outburst floods that inundated the Lajia site and sent the shockwave thousands of kilometres downstream on the Central Plains, directly responsible for the founding of the legendary Xia Dynasty. The scholarly backlash to this bold opinion, itself a massive shockwave, objects that the floods were not directly linked to the earthquake; but rather, these were flash floods and mudflows caused by excessive rainfall during the time. It was the combination of these meteorological events and the earthquakes that took place before and after them that eventually caused the toll of this once flourishing community at Lajia, burying its houses and fields (Wang et al., 2021a; Wu Q. et al., 2016; Zhang Y. et al., 2019).

Parallel to the He-Huang basins, to the west lies the Hexi Corridor, a long and narrow strip of arable land nestled between the Qinghai-Tibetan and Mongolian plateaus. Flanked by a range of mountains, the corridor is filled with small river basins and fluvial fans and encroached by deserts. Analysis of lacustrine sediments located along the corridor reveals a warm and humid early-to-middle-Holocene climate and a prolonged aridification from ca. 5,000BP onwards. During the late Holocene, the weakening Asian summer monsoon resulted in the Westerlies system dominating the climate in the western stretch of the corridor, which might have contributed to the delayed timing of lake shrinkage and desiccation of river channels (Li X. Q. et al., 2013; Wang et al., 2017; Zhao et al., 2015). Some small rivers, such as the Heihe 黑河 River, experienced an anti-phasing change in hydrology during the middle-to-late Holocene (Herzschuh et al., 2004), displaying a relatively high water table. The patchy vegetation mainly comprised of sparse desert-grassland species, although better vegetation could be found around many lakes and oases (Mao et al., 2007; Zheng et al., 2006). As harsh and dry it might look today, these lakes, oases, and rivers during humid spells of the Holocene would have become vital sources for prehistoric occupation and facilitating regional interactions.

The corridor saw a westward migration of the Yangshao-Majiayao people from the He-Huang region. This migration reached the western end of the region by the late-Majiayao phase (ca. 4,500BP), although its presence in the western frontiers was scattered. After a 'quiet' Banshan 半山 phase (4,500–4,300BP), the region became a bustling place during the Machang (4,300–4,000BP) and succeeding cultural phases (Gao et al., 2019; Li et al., 2010) (Figure 9). The diverse cultivars that arrived during this unprecedented wave of prehistoric migration in the corridor have been spotlight of recent environmental and archaeological surveys that aim to disentangle 'food globalisation' in prehistory (Dong et al., 2022; Jones et al., 2011). These cultivars came from the Central Plains in the East and the Eurasian continent in the West, through mountains and valley routes. Albeit of limited quantity, archaeobotanical remains from late-Yangshao sites in the eastern Ganqing 甘青 region demonstrate the practice of dryland millet farming driving the westward spread of millet farming (Guo et al., 2023). Continuing this trend, Majiayao farmers established their farms mostly on low-altitude terraces, where optimal soil and water conditions can be sought (Dong et al., 2018). Sheep herding might have also appeared but only played a minor role in subsistence economies (Han, 2008: 137). By the Machang phase (4,300–4,000BP), the developed millet farming is manifested by the high-density settlement distribution, high-level utilisation of arable land, and sufficient water along rivers (Wang L. et al., 2014). Around 4,000BP, the climate became much drier. Many sites were surrounded by expanding deserts and a series of socio-economic adjustments took place. Riverine sites were abandoned as there was simply no water in the river; some sites began to move to high-altitude places and adopted pastoral lifestyles; and the once widespread Machang-culture sites also suffered a clear contraction (Gao et al., 2019).

During the succeeding Qijia culture and Siba 四坝 culture (3,900–3,500BP), a multi-cropping system was established, which was continuously dominated by millet farming but supplemented by some introduced crops coming from Southwest Asia and nearby regions such as Tibet (e.g., hull-less barley). The spatiotemporal variations of these introduced crops illustrate their great adaptability in new environments and their potentially variable roles in the society. Despite dry conditions around 4,000BP, millets remained the dominant crop for their high yield and low water requirement. After 4,000BP, wheat-and-barley farming began to spread in western and central Gansu (Dong et al., 2018; Stevens et al., 2016). Isotopic evidence suggests a distinctive dietary shift from a C_4-based (millet) food consumption to one that consisted of both C_4 and C_3-based (most likely from wheat and possibly barley) foods during this time (Liu X. et al., 2014; Ma et al., 2016). The adoption of new crops, especially wheat, seemed to be rapid and the consumption of them seemed to be of a relatively larger scale. Reasons for such changes are much speculated. The higher yield of wheat and potentially barley per hectare would have certainly made them more advantageous than millets (Liu X. et al., 2014). However, wheat farming requires more water to grow, which might not have been a problem in those desert oases or spots with good sources of water such as snowmelt in the spring and winter. The late-Neolithic wheat-and-barley farmers might have adopted special strategies of water management to sustain yields (Li et al., 2022). In the Zhuanglang 庄浪 Basin, sites yielding more wheat than barley were often located close to rivers and springs whilst sites with predominant barley remains tended to be situated on higher-altitude hills. The resilience of barley to diverse environmental conditions is recently revealed by genetic studies (Lister et al., 2018), which was crucial to its spread across arid landscapes. The shift to wheat-and-barley farming might have also stemmed from complex cultural changes at this hotspot of trans-Eurasian interactions, especially when compared with the contemporary farming system in eastern Gansu, which was still dominated by millet farming (Chen T. et al., 2019).

Underpinning these movements of early cultivators are exchanges of technologies, ideas, and goods, which transformed prehistoric and historic lives in the Hexi Corridor and beyond (Flad, 2023). Metal objects already occurred in the Majiayao culture, but their dates and casting technologies remain subjects of debates. However, the succeeding Qijia and Siba cultures saw a boom in metal casting industry, forming the so-called metallurgical entity (Chen, 2017a). Although copper objects that contained different trace elements continued to account for a substantial proportion in many excavated metal assemblages, the appearance of tin-, lead-, and arsenic-bronzes suggests a leap forward in bronze casting, as early casters actively experimented new knowledge (e.g., arsenic-bronzes probably influenced by the west) and skills. The corridor was not just a region of technological transmission but a hub of indigenous innovations. Sparks of casting activities spread across the corridor and some sites even became centres of bronze production (Chen, 2017b). The shining objects began to be favoured by the local residents and their neighbours; more new forms and categories of metals were created (Chen, 2017b; Chen et al., 2018; Pan and Shui, 2020). As it developed and spread, the casting technology also diversified and diverged. For instance, arsenic bronzes mostly occurred in the eastern corridor, whilst tin-bronzes were more common in the western region in the early stage. By the late stage, tin-bronzes gradually became dominant (Li and Shui, 2000; Sun et al., 2003). The region's rich sources of stones, including some precious stones, also fostered a burgeoning industry of stone and jade production. Recent evidence suggests that a group of people were engaged in systematic exploitation of jade mines in the region as early as 4,000BP (Chen and Yang, 2021; Chen et al., 2021), triggering an expanding scale of production. A single burial at the Huangniangniangtai 皇娘娘台 cemetery could contain dozens of stone *bi* 璧 discs, alongside elaborate painted-pottery vessels. The usage of *bi* and *cong* 琮 tubes in Qijia contexts might have been influenced by the Taosi and other cultures far in the east (Han, 2008: 152), facilitated by long-distance connections between the corridor and the Loess Plateau.

The region's rich sources of metal ores (e.g., Tang and Bai, 2000) and other natural resources, its pioneering technology, and super connectivity became a driving wheel for radical changes. Through participation in the production, distribution, and consumption as well as exchange of luxurious goods, some groups would have gained prestigious social status. For others, the consumption of these goods alongside other perishable products such as wheat or pigs and sheep was part of their continuous effort to establish and consolidate regional networks, involving feasting and ceremonious activities such as divination (Flad et al., 2008). The region had become a centre of intensive communication and competition for resources, technologies, and goods (Zhang, 2017), and more changes were on the horizon.

The Hetao Plain and the Jin-Shaanxi Plateau: Formation and Change of the Agropastoralism Sphere

As the Yellow River enters China's second tier, it embarks on a spectacular adventure. The river meanders through rocky terrains and basins in a narrow belt of the Hetao Plain (Figure 10a). The environment looks tranquil today, but its Quaternary history was wrought with tectonic movements, active channel migration and deposition, and frequent dust storms. The widespread and thick limnetic and alluvial sediments deposited during the middle-to-late Pleistocene resulted in a complicated regional hydrology, marked by 'broken rivers' and highly bifurcated branches that fed many lakes and wetlands and nourished fertile land.

The self-enclosed Daihai 岱海 Lake basin contains a lake ca. 160 km^2 in size and a drainage area of ca. 2,300 km^2. Reconstruction of Holocene lake level showed that the lake enjoyed an expansion and high water level during the late Holocene. This favourable hydrological regime is different from other regions that underwent aridification. Additionally, the basin also developed alluvial fans on mountain piedmonts, with organic-rich sediments on the distal fans, which were conducive to farming activities. Despite conflicting results from different pollen studies, some records reveal a noticeable expansion of coniferous and broadleaved species between 6,700–3,500BP in the basin, benefiting from the

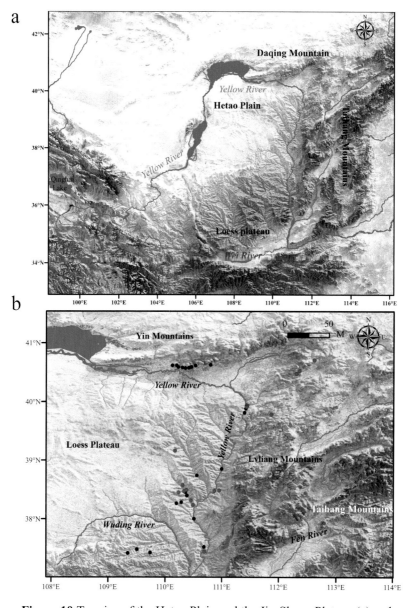

Figure 10 Terrains of the Hetao Plain and the Jin-Shaan Plateau (a) and late-prehistoric sites in the region (b). Black and red dots refer to Miaodigou-II-period sites and Longshan-period sites, respectively, site data from Song and Zhang (2022).

optimal humidity (Sun et al., 2006). Even for those records that show a lushing middle-Holocene broadleaved vegetation followed by a drier-and-colder pollen assemblage from ca. 4,500BP, the middle-late-Holocene transition did not coincide with a steady decline of vegetation cover but was punctuated by a humid episode with abundant arboreal pollen (>20 per cent) in a forest-steppe environment (Xiao et al., 2004; Xu et al., 2010). According to Sun et al. (2022), vegetation cover in the Daihai basin remained stable until 5,100BP, dominated by deciduous forest of *Quercus, Betula*, and *Pinus*, and whilst vegetation cover started to decline after 5,100BP, the change might be partly attributed to human activities, with evidence of increasing frequencies of fire related to land-use history during the Yangshao and later periods (Wang et al., 2013). The environment and landscape of prehistoric Daihai Lake basin are not unique. There were hundreds of small, closed lakes in the Daqingshan 大青山 Mountain and Huangqihai 黄旗海 Lake basin, many of which were sustained by a high lake level between ca. 6,000–3,800BP (Yang, 2001; Zhao, 2011).

Apart from the lakes, the middle-to-late Holocene landscape in the Hetao Plain was dominated by mosaics of deserts, sand dunes, and mountains. The southern piedmonts of the Daqingshan Mountains (Figure 10b) developed distinctive fluvial fans during the Holocene, circumvented by incised gullies (Ma et al., 1999; Zhang et al., 2020). These fans aligned regularly from east to west like a string of beads protruding from the mountain fronts. As expected, many of these fans contained fertile soils (Yin et al., 2005) that would have promoted vegetation growth. Even in the deserts, patches of soil developed during the warm and humid periods of the Holocene can be commonly found (Jin et al., 2001).

Compared to the heterogeneous landscape of the Hetao Plain, the Jin-Shaan Plateau has more homogeneous landforms. Situated at the heartland of the Loess Plateau, the Jin-Shaan Plateau has massive loess deposition reaching several hundred metres in thickness. After making a dramatic U-turn, the Yellow River channel began cutting through the massive Jin-Shaan Plateau in another spectacular journey. Responding to tectonic elevation and base-level changes, the river incision created a gigantic canyon that split the plateau into vast loess land on both sides of the river. Along the Yellow River channel and its tributaries lie the picturesque multi-ordered terraces, caused by the continuous alluvial incision. Some stand almost 200 m high on the loess cliff. Recent studies have also shown that, after a prolonged stability, tributary channels experienced further incision ca. 6,000–5,000BP before starting to aggrade, forming younger-age terraces (Cheng et al., 1998). Located on these terrace surfaces are many Palaeolithic and Neolithic sites (e.g., Longwangchan 龙王辿).

There were also several basins located deep in the loess land that were home to growing Neolithic populations. For instance, the Datong 大同 Basin and Xinding 忻定 Basin are situated in a descending order from north to south at 1,100–1,000 masl and 1,000–800 masl, respectively. The Datong Basin became a large lake that fed into several regional rivers in its east during the Pleistocene. Pleistocene deposits in the centre of the basin are dominated by lacustrine sediments whereas the edges comprise gravels and wind-blown loess. Sedimentation mostly ceased during the Holocene, leaving the basin being incised by rivers (Yang, 2015: 13). On the left of the plateau in Shaanxi, although the vast high loess land is more open with an evident lack of massive enclosed basins, the landscape is similarly subject to profound alteration by rivers. In many tributary catchments, the closer to the rivers, the deeper the incision reaches whilst the landform becomes gentler towards the upstream.

As a whole, the middle to late Holocene landscape of the Jin-Shaan Plateau was dominated by loess tablelands, high and low terraces, alluvial lowlands, and inland basins. The Holocene vegetation in the region was dominated by sparse steppe-grassland species. Whilst the percentage of deciduous-broadleaved species and hygrophilous plants and ferns increased during some warm spells (e.g., 7,000–4,000BP), they never became dominant (Fan et al., 2007). The hydrological regime of the plateau is generally dry, with a deep groundwater table and scattered surface water. Prehistoric communities would have relied heavily on river water, springs, and other forms of surface water if they had not effectively utilised groundwater. Drastic measures were required to tackle critical challenge on water in the Jin-Shaan Plateau, but such evidence is not yet available.

In the Hetao Plain, the aforementioned optimal locations provided much-needed sanctuaries for Holocene human settlements. The region's Neolithic inhabitation oscillated at a pace that was intrinsically linked to the ecological changes described earlier. The region was a busy place with the Shihushan 石虎山 culture (ca. 6,800–6,200BP) and contemporary groups (e.g., the Lujiapo 鲁家坡 type culture) living in diverse landforms (Fu, 2017). From ca. 5,000BP, stone-walled sites first appeared on the southern piedmonts of the Daqingshan Mountains (Dai, 2016). They were strategically located and clustered in small groups, mostly on piedmont fronts several dozen metres higher than the alluvial plains. Each cluster consisted of 2–3 sites and was 4–5 km apart. Strikingly, the sites shared many common features, such as architectural technologies and settlement layout. The latter emphasised similar domestic designs and ritual infrastructures (e.g., altars). Almost contemporaneously, another group of stone-walled sites emerged on the two banks of the Yellow River in eastern Ordos, displaying similar settlement features to those in Daqingshan with a common emphasis on defence.

These phenomena imply that social units formed internally egalitarian groups at a time of escalating external competition for natural resources and conflicts among different communities.

This trend intensified in the following millennia (ca. 4,500–4,200BP). Settlements in the Eastern Ordos continued to thrive, whilst the Daihai Lake basin became a place of settlement congregation. These sites were situated on slopes and low hills, forming at least the eastern and western clusters of ca. 40 sites on slopes and low hills along the lake and rivers. Many of them adopted new architectural techniques, such as building cave houses with lime-plastered floors, whilst inheriting the stone wall tradition. The walls were built on gully cliffs and rolling terrains, an indicator of the local residents' concern for defence. Similarly, some houses were built on bare rocky surface, with uniform orientation and design. These common architectural technologies and settlement layouts enhanced the collective identity between different groups within the settlement when the external environment became more hostile. By the latter half of the Longshan period (ca. 4,200–3,800BP), the region became an arena for radical social developments, with the phenomenal rise of the Shimao 石峁 walled site and its contemporaries in the Yulin region (Figure 11a) whilst settlements in Daihai and eastern Ordos had either disappeared or suffered a decline (Dai, 2016). The Shimao site reached an enormous size of 400 ha and its complicated stone-walled structure and stepped-cliff-like monuments (Figure 12a) represent an extraordinary effort to reorganise resources, labour, and power as competition and conflict within and between different regions became fiercer. The elaborate and awe-inspiring design and decoration of the recently excavated eastern gate, the chilling fact that most of the beheaded skulls in two sacrificial pits found near the gate were female, and the magnificent 8 ha Huangchengtai 皇城台 platform in the centre of Shimao (Jaang et al., 2018; Sun et al., 2018), all tell the great successes and tragedies that the Shimao people and its contemporaries had to experience.

Some contemporary sites of Shimao are found on the edge, or in the middle of desert or mobile sand dunes in an extraordinary move to optimise the use of land and other resources in the region (e.g., Huoshiliang 火石梁, Muzhuzhuliang 木柱柱梁, and Xinhua 新华, Figure 11). A radical shift from a typical millet-pig agricultural lifestyle during the late-Yangshao period to an agropastoral economy that incorporated new cultivars occurred (Hu S. M. et al., 2022). In some faunal assemblages, domesticated sheep and cattle account for up to 60 per cent. These developments marked an economic diversification characterised by a less prominent differentiation of meat acquisition strategies between the 'urban' and 'rural' sites (Owlett et al., 2018), which is further interpreted as a form of self-sufficient meat production without specialisation.

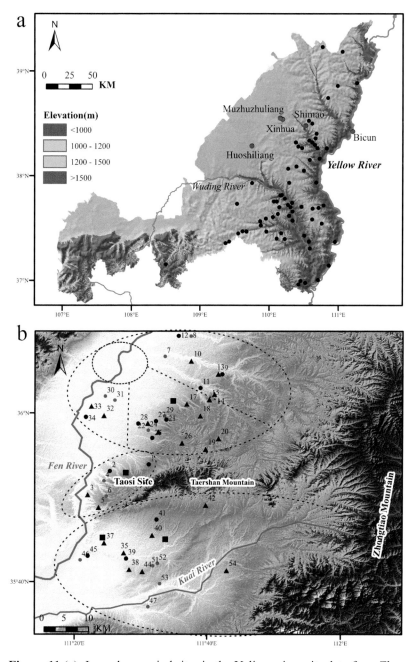

Figure 11 (a): Longshan-period sites in the Yulin region, site date from Zhao (2021). (b): Longshan-period sites surrounding Taosi; squares, triangles, and dots indicate large-, medium-, and small-sized sites, respectively. Site data from He (2011).

a

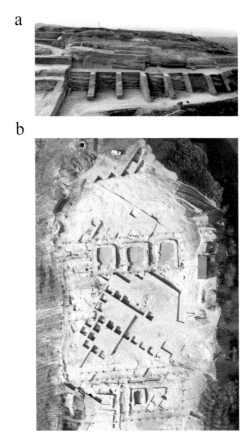

b

Figure 12 (a): Excavation of the Huangchengtai Platform foundation at Shimao, after Sun et al. (2020). (b): Excavation of the Dayingpanliang location at Lushanmao, after Ma et al. (2019).

Plant remains from many more sites reveal different crop choices. Meanwhile, people's understanding of millet farming became more sophisticated. At Shimao, foxtail millet gradually became more favoured over broomcorn millet from the late-Longshan period to the succeeding 'Xia' period, even though broomcorn millet is known as a robust crop in harsh growing conditions (Sheng et al., 2021). A range of plants might be also cultivated as fodder. The presence of rice and soybean was likely acquired through exchange with neighbours. These strategies are vividly described as 'hard to part with agriculture and impossible to live without pastoralism' at Shimao (Yang et al., 2022: 101), contrasting with those at small-sized sites focusing on a few more crops, such as broomcorn millet (Sheng et al., 2020) which is often cultivated at frontier locations with poor soil conditions.

The economic and dietary developments brought about profound changes in society. Social gatherings involving wine drinking might be held at Shimao's eastern gate and possibly other locations (Liu et al., 2022). Rice and other cereals, whether traded in or locally cultivated, were utilised to produce the wine, and new cooking sets were invented to cater the culinary and ceremonial needs. Mortuary and settlement data indicate a distinct social stratification within and between Shimao and its many neighbours. Interestingly, as competition remained intense, settlement structures and architecture technologies in the region also started to diverge. A notable example for comparison was the Lushanmao 芦山峁 site (4,300–4,200BP), where large monuments were built primarily by the pounded-earth technology without stones (Ma et al., 2019), different from the Shimao's stone-and-earth architecture (Figure 12b). At other sites, such as Muzhuzhuliang, multiple moats were dug (SPIA, 2015). This regional differentiation in settlement structure and architecture is another indication of the late-Neolithic people's diverse and robust adaptations to the environment.

Influence of these remarkable changes started to radiate outward, and ripple of technological and economic developments began to be felt across the Hetao and Jinshan regions. Such a powerful force expanded all the way south, causing series collisions and conflicts. Scholars relish the sensational encounter between Shimao and Taosi, but there are many important sites situated in the vast, intermediate landmass between them. Indeed, the stories of their interactions are far more complicated than scholars have been able to depict.

Houchengzui 后城咀 (ca. 4,000BP) and Bicun 碧村 (4,200–3,800BP) are two such important sites (Figure 11a). Located 20 km east of the Yellow River, Houchengzui measures ca. 140 ha. Its impressive defence system includes stone walls, gates, bastions, *wengcheng* towers, moats, and other affiliated facilities (Dang and Sun, 2022). Such a sophisticated design is mirrored at Bicun. Situated at the confluence of the Weifen 渭汾 River and the Yellow River, the Bicun walled site's strategical location is convenient to both defence and communication. Three sides of it were encircled by cliffs, whilst one side was connected to the loess inland, which is >100 m higher than the valley bottom (Figure 13a). The terrace that stands high above the river already existed during the Longshan period, but its size was limited, and the Bicun people therefore opted to build their multiple-ringed walls on still higher-up loess tableland to obtain more land, better security, and easier transportation (Wang et al., 2021b; Zhang, 2023). Even today, despite severe erosion, the arable land on the tableland is significantly larger than other locations (Zhu, 1989). Flotation results show an established dryland farming in the region, dominated by foxtail and broomcorn millets (Jiang et al., 2019; also see Hou et al., 2023 for isotopic

a b

Figure 13 (a): Geographic location of the Bicun site on the loess *liang* tableland, with the Hun River on the right (the Yellow River is not shown in the photo), photo courtesy of Dr. Hui Wang. (b): Erosion gully around Xiaweiluo, by the edges of the cliffs are the Longshan-period cave houses.

results that suggest the same). However, the trade-off for this settlement choice might have been constant water shortage on high loess land. Not only was water from rivers and springs meagre, but the groundwater table was also generally low, even during warm and humid periods. Evidence of how people utilised water remains hard to trace. The discoveries of a pond on Huangchengtai at Shimao and an architectural complex at Lushanmao (Ma et al., 2019; Sun et al., 2020) are just a tip of the iceberg of the potentially diverse strategies adopted by the Longshan populations to sustain long-term water usage, which would have in turn had a profound impact on regional settlements and economic structure. Some would stick to millet farming whilst others were ready to take the risk and adapt to changing situations with new opportunities.

The environmental, settlement and economic characteristics discussed in the preceding paragraphs were foundations that enabled the Hetao Plain and Jin-Shaan Plateau to play a pivotal role in mediating and promoting regional communications in late-prehistoric North China. Regional transportation was confined mostly on the high but generally flat loess land as the low yet discontinuous and often erosive riverine valleys were unsuitable for easy transportation. People were moving frequently and far, and things and ideas were spreading fast on the loess land (e.g., Han, 2008: 182). The stone-walled sites, earthen-monument sites, and other sites surrounding them constituted distinct cultural landscapes in the Hetao Plain and Jin-Shaan Plateau, supported by adaptable agropastoral economies. They interacted with their neighbours such as Taosi through different mechanisms and highly fluid yet porous boundaries. In the next phase of intensive interactions between China and its western neighbours, these places were a major intermediary for horse and population movements as land became drier (cf. Rawson, 2023).

The Fen-Wei Basin: Rival of Hetao and Jin-shan Plateaus

As one of the most populous regions, the Fen-Wei Basin has exceptional fertile soils, mild climate, and inhabitable landforms (Figure 14). Some of the Yellow River's largest tributaries flow through the region, continuing to fill up the massive Fenwei rift which was ruptured millions of years ago, and creating a string of alluvial basins that are like beads in a multi-strand necklace, including the Taiyuan Basin, the Linfen Basin, and the Guanzhong Basin. Taiyuan and Linfen Basins formed different alluvial landscapes. In the former, alluvial incision during the early Holocene gradually cut the land into tablelands and other land units on the edge of the basin. Some of the incised valleys were up to 20 m deep. Alluvial aggradation followed, forming several fill terraces in the central and eastern parts of the basin. Conversely, because of its location further downstream, the Linfen Basin experienced a more prolonged period of river downcutting during the late Pleistocene and Holocene, resulting in massive gullies (30–40 m deep) which were never fully filled up again. The terraces that formed on such landforms were characterised by high altitude, good drainage, and stable surface conditions.

The geomorphological processes just described resulted in distinctive settlement distribution patterns in the basins. In the Taiyuan Basin, most prehistoric sites were located on the tablelands along the basin's edge, whilst the central part

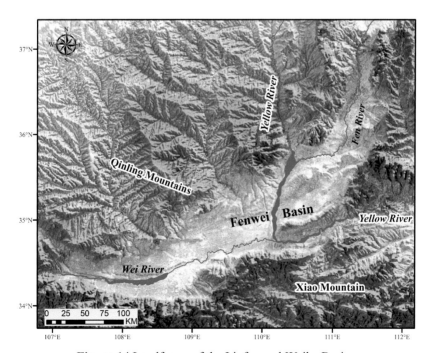

Figure 14 Landforms of the Linfen and Weihe Basins.

of the basin remained uninhabitable due to its unstable geomorphological and hydrological conditions. This resulted in the so-called 'around-basin' distribution mode, in contrast to the 'full-basin' distribution mode in the Linfen Basin. In the latter, most archaeological sites were situated on platform-type plains and loess tablelands across the basin. Recent surveys have shown that from late-Yangshao period (ca. 5,500BP) onwards, the settlement number saw a significant decline in the Linfen Basin from >140 sites to ca. 50 sites, whilst that in the Taiyuan Basin increased from 17 to 35. This change is tentatively interpreted as due to a decline of 'land carrying capacity' in the Linfen Basin which drove a demographic shift to the Taiyuan Basin and other regions. This assertion remains questionable as the settlement number increased to 175 again by the Miaodigou 庙底沟-II (4,700–4,300BP) and to >230 by the Longshan period (4,300–3,800BP) in the Linfen Basin (Figure 15a–c) (Lü et al., 2019).

The Longshan period in Linfen coincided with a warm climate, despite a lower-level humidity. Over 230 sites were concentrated in at least eight clusters. Each cluster contained four to five-tiered settlements centred around one large site ranging in size from 50 to 100 ha or 100 to 300 ha (Figure 11b). The majority of these sites spread across the two banks of the Fen River, on average 2 km apart. This unprecedented boom of Longshan settlements benefited from the existence of some lakes and wetlands at the time (He, 2013). Linfen became a nexus of socio-economic developments, culminating in the rise of the Taosi walled site. Taosi sits on a loess *yuan* tableland which gradually transitions to the piedmont of the Tao'ershan 塔儿山 Mountains. This environment offered everything Taosi needed. The *yuan* surface provided fertile soil for agricultural growth and was ideal for large-scale earthen construction. The Nan 南 River already flew south of the site. The Fen River was not very far but also not close enough to cause floods. Together with the nearby limestone outcrops and several shallow ditches, these rivers must have been the main source of water. The mountains provided timber and stones, including those used for lime production (Li T. Y. et al., 2013).

Taosi began as a modest settlement but quickly grew to an earthen-walled town (100 ha) at ca. 4,300BP. It continued to expand and eventually became an enormous regional centre, covering 280 ha. The site's sophisticated layout included roads running regularly across the enclosed area, and several quadrants are believed to have specialised economic or other functions. Monuments, cemeteries, and ceremonial places were also present, some of which were enclosed by separate earthen walls. Of the most conspicuous was the 'observatory' located in the southeast. Despite continuing controversy (e.g., Liu and Chen, 2012), the discovery of human sacrifices and surrounding offerings and the lack of daily-life wastes confirm the uniqueness and restricted access of the locale. Privileged or

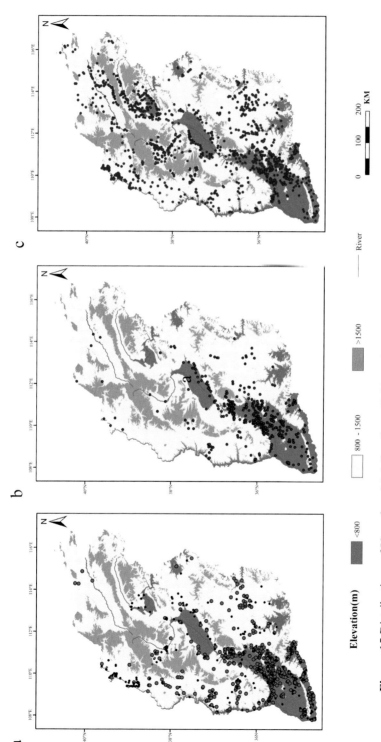

Figure 15 Distributions of Yangshao (a), Miaodiogu-II (b), and Longshan (c)-period sites in the Taiyuan and Linfen Basins, site data from Hosner et al. (2016). Left image: red, blue, and black dots refer to early-, middle-, and late-Yangshao-period sites, respectively.

specialised groups must have been visiting this vicinity regularly for ceremonial activities, where some of the most extravagant tombs in late-prehistoric China were found (He, 2013). Tomb no. IIM22 has massive tomb space with many niches and abundant luxurious burial goods that were either locally produced or acquired from long-distance exchange. The staggering contrast between these 'royal' tombs and ordinary ones indicates a clear social stratification closely tied to the highly developed agriculture, craft production, and regional exchange.

Taosi craftsmen procured stone raw materials from nearby locations and might have monopolised quarries such as the Dagudui 大崮堆 Mountain. Although the ample supply of stones led to a small-scale production 'lack of technological sophistication' at Taosi, the abundant tools it produced were sufficient for both 'on-site uses' and exports (Liu et al., 2013). This might represent only a small fraction of the expanding craft production industries, through which natural resources and labourers in the region were pulled together (possibly under diverse organisations and governance structures) (cf. Flad, 2018) and contributed to the early urbanisation. The urbanisation could not have been achieved without agricultural prosperity. Agriculture at Taosi relied overwhelmingly on foxtail millets, but the presence of a few rice grains in the floral assemblage raises the possibility of local rice cultivation (Zhao and He, 2006). The latter was not impossible as rice has been found at several other sites in the region too (e.g., Zhoujiazhuang 周家庄) (Jiang et al., 2019) and there is evidence that some elites or high-status people might consume more rice than others (SPIA et al., 2016). Pigs were the main source of meat at Taosi. Halved, whole pigs and mandibles were frequently consumed on mortuary occasions (IACASS and LMBCR, 2015; Xia and Gao, 2022). Domesticated cattle and sheep were also raised with various strategies (Chen X. L. et al., 2012; Yang et al., 2023). Some sheep might have been used for wool production, which, if true, is one of earliest evidence of secondary animal production in prehistoric China (Brunson et al., 2015).

Taosi and its contemporaries represent a pinnacle of remarkable adaptations to the vast loess environment. They inherited strong economic foundation from the preceding late-Yangshao period, which produced ample millets and pigs to be consumed on ordinary and special social events. They embraced new technologies (e.g., painted pottery and lacquer technologies) and adapted them to their own purposes. They harnessed and transformed the loess environment into a prosperous land that benefited from their successful dryland farming, clever water-usage techniques (e.g., wells, Wang, 2001), earthen-architecture building (He, 2013), and efficient transportation systems. These interactions were multi-directional. Jade and bronzes and other luxurious goods were circulated among the elites or certain social groups. Equally important was the frequent circulation of many other goods, including common ceramic products from as far as Shandong in the east and Middle Yangtze River, as well as ideas, lifestyles, and beliefs, which permeated into different levels of society and stimulated region-wide changes (Zhang H., 2022).

However, Taosi eventually declined. By the late phase, the site area had contracted, and many buildings were abandoned. Whilst it is popularly speculated that external force such as the 'invasion' by Shimao caused its demise, intensified human land use in the region had left a noticeable impact on the environment. This would have exacerbated the erosion process that had already created some gullies around the site and contributed to or even accelerated the drastic socio-economic changes at the end of Taosi (Yang, 2004).

The Yuncheng Basin situated south of the Linfen Basin emerged as another centre of socio-economic developments during the Longshan period (Figure 15). The basin is home to several mega-sized Longshan sites, including Zhoujiazhuang and Sili-Potou 寺里-坡头 (Jiang and Tian, 2023; SPIA et al., 2004), which were strategically located to connect different parts of the Loess Plateau and the Yellow River basins, and in close proximity to key natural resources, notably salt. Some of the sites might have actively involved in the production and trade of salt and other products such as jade and probably cinnabar (Fang, 2023), and become great rivals of Taosi (Dai, 2021). Occupants of these sites amassed substantial wealth, leading to the development of significant social stratification as evidenced by the rich burials with jade and human sacrifices at the Qingliangsi 清凉寺 cemetery (SPIA et al., 2016).

Stretching along the Yellow River, the Yuncheng Basin then gradually transitions to the Wei River (Guanzhong) Basin in the southwest (Figure 15). As the largest tributary of the Yellow River, the Wei River contributes 16 per cent of the water and almost 1/3 of the sediments in the Lower Yellow River, winding its way along the Loess Plateau and the Qinling Mountains. The geological graben rifted the Guanzhong Basin and created an enormous accommodating space, protected by the Qinling Mountains to the south, which continues to receive wind-blown dust and alluvial sediments. Combined with widespread surface erosion, these processes create characteristic loess and alluvial landforms. The former includes typical *yuan*, *liang*, and *mao* tablelands, most of which stand to the north of the Wei River, including some famous ones such as the Wuzhang 五丈, Shenhe 神禾, and Bailu 白鹿 *yuans* that were historical arenas of intensive economic activities and political events. Bailu *yuan*, for instance, rises 780–680 masl with a massive relative height of 150–320 m against the Ba 灞 River, spanning ca. 25 km from west to east, and ca. 6–10 km from north to south. The tableland surface continues to be incised by surface runoff into smaller land units, which are demarcated by massive erosion gullies often several dozens or hundreds of metres deep.

Hancheng and Tongchuan, located further north and bordering the southern tip of the Jin-Shaan Plateau, also possess fertile loess land similar to that of Guanzhong, whereas further south in the region are alluvial terraces and plains that extend for several hundred kilometres along the Wei River channel and its tributaries. The river is contained in a long but narrow stretch in the basin, carving out multiple alluvial terraces. Relatively young terraces formed since the late Pleistocene are ca. 20 m higher than the river water, making them ideal locations for settlement. Following the prosperous Yangshao period, with a staggering number of some 1,000 sites, significant changes occurred during the Longshan period (ca. 4,500–3,900BP) in the Guanzhong Basin (Figure 16a). First, the number of Longshan-period settlements, belonging to several different local types (Liang, 1994), declined noticeably, coinciding particularly with the abandonment of many Yangshao culture sites in alluvial lowlands. However, recent surveys also showed that the Longshan-period settlements continued to thrive in the Zhouyuan area in western Guanzhong (ZAT, 2005, 2010; Zhang X. H., 2013). Second, whilst there is a general trend of relocating to high-altitude places such as the loess tablelands, the Longshan people also started to diversify their living environments, best illustrated by a spatial analysis of settlement distribution in many tributary basins (Ma, 2010: 36). For instance, in the Chan 浐 and Ba River basin, although the number of Longshan-period settlements reduced to ca. 40 (from 52 during the latter phase of the Yangshao culture), these settlements were located as high up as the mountain piedmonts and as low down as riverine places (Shao, 2009: 56). Third, these changes indicate that the spatial and temporal variations of the Yangshao-Longshan settlements are very patchy within and between different tributary basins. In the Qishui 漆水 River valley, for example, the decline of Longshan-period settlements is more evident in the western part of the basin than in the eastern part, but overall not as dramatic as in other regions (Jiang and Cui, 2017). The Longshan sites were situated further away from the rivers and were generally smaller in size.

The Longshan migration to higher-altitude environments cannot be simply explained as a strategy to prevent floods. Rather, it was facilitated by a range of technological innovations, including the construction of cave houses (*yaodong* 窑洞), the cave-like residential units in the loess area. Prehistoric forms of cave houses have been unearthed in recent excavations. Whilst already occurring during the late-Yangshao period in central Guanzhong (e.g., at Yangguanzhai 杨官寨), cave houses became a more prominent component of Longshan-period settlements on the loess highlands (Zhang C., 2022) (Figure 16b). They are mostly homogeneous in design, often consisting of a rear room, front room, and a courtyard, and can accommodate a single nucleated family,

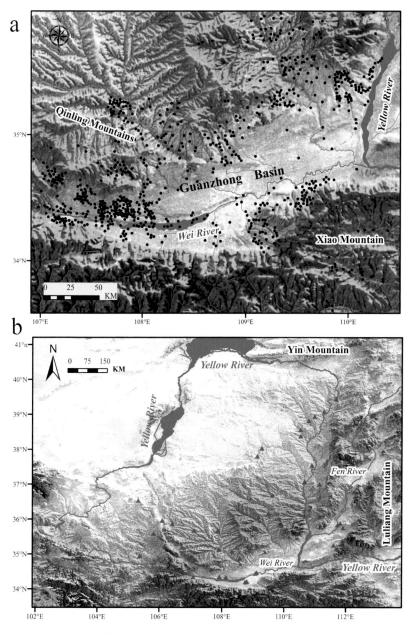

Figure 16 (a): Distributions of Longshan-period sites in the Guanzhong Basin, site data from Hosner et al. (2016). (b): Location of late-prehistoric sites where cave houses have been found, site data from Wang (in press).

although more variant forms gradually developed. Construction of cave houses followed similar procedures: a chamber would be bored horizontally into a vertical loess cliff, followed by the careful embellishment of the domestic space with lime-pastered floor, lower part of the wall, and hearth (Figure 17a). Cave house is considered a precursor of the 'front-hall-and-rear-room' living mode in the increasingly cold environment (Sun and Shao, 2018). Constructing them required much less timber, and their engineering design resonated with the distinctive upward cleavage of the loess; their placement in cliffs suited

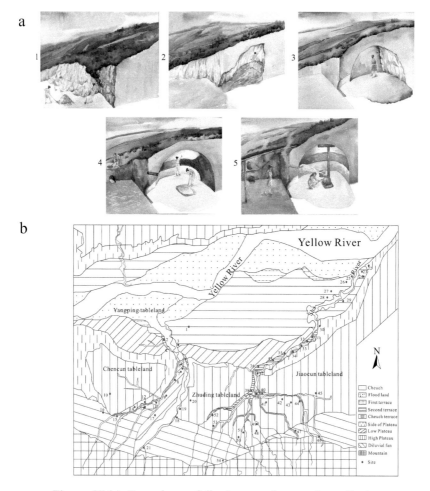

Figure 17 (a): Procedures of digging cave houses, from digging the cliff (1), horizontal boring (2), finishing off the wall (3), interior decoration (4), and to use (5), after Sun and Shao (2018). (b) Geomorphology and distributions of Neolithic sites in the Zhuding *yuan* loess tableland in Lingbao, Henan, after Wei and Zhang (2017).

perfectly with the loess landform. With these advantages, cave house fostered a new eco-cultural system at a time of escalating environmental and climatic crises (e.g., gullies created by increased erosion).

The prevalence of cave house dwellings also extended to larger settlements. Although the total number and overall structure of larger settlements in Guanzhong are unclear compared to other neighbouring regions, the Taiping 太平 site (4,150–3,700BP) is an exception. Unlike Taosi or Shimao, the site (measuring ca. 100 ha) is situated much closer to the alluvial lowland, and the presence of multiple moats indicates the importance of drainage. Cave houses were a common feature among other architectural styles at Taiping (Wang, in press). Just as cave houses being favoured for their design and cultural taste by contemporary society, even in places without suitable cliffs for digging the caves, they too became so deeply entrenched in Longshan society on the Loess Plateau that the adoption of them transcended beyond environmental reasons.

Residents of both small and large Longshan-period sites in Guanzhong engaged in similar agricultural activities as their neighbours, making the most of what the loess motherland had to offer (Chen, 2020; Liu et al., 2001). Although rice might be cultivated and wheat also occurred at some sites (Wang X. et al., 2015; ZAT, 2004), they were both of less importance. Because of its unique geographic location, the Guanzhong Basin was susceptible to strong external influences. Future research might reveal the introduction of bronze casting technology through Longshan-culture agents such as the Keshengzhuang 客省庄-II culture to the Central Plains. The possible routes for this important technological transmission might be those valleys corridors that connected the region with the steppes, the Central Plains, and northwest China.

Just as the origins of the Shaanxi Longshan culture are enigmatic, the end of it is clouded by myths too. Some Longshan culture sites in small tributaries (e.g., the Qishui River) are found overlain by flood deposits. It is suggested that region-wide floods during the early phase of the late-Longshan period (ca. 4,300–4,000BP) wiped out many low-altitude sites whilst those situated on high terraces and loess *yuan* tablelands flourished during the late-Longshan phase (Huang et al., 2011). However, such propositions are problematic not least because the chronologies (with 100–200 years of uncertainty, Huang et al., 2012) related to the floods and the archaeological cultures are too crude to allow for a comfortable superimposition of these events. Floods might have been widespread and devastating in late Holocene North China, but epitomising the causal relationship between floods and historical events remains too difficult a task to be tackled by any single discipline.

The loess landforms are under constant alteration by incision of the Yellow River. After passing the Sanmenxia Gorge, the river unleashes its long-constrained water onto the North China Plains. The basic landforms around Sanmenxia include fluvial fans on piedmont fronts, loess hills and tablelands, and alluvial terraces and plains (Figure 17b). The first two are prevalent, whilst the latter are mostly restricted to the narrow strip between the Yellow River and the loess highlands. Scattered between these landforms are many second-order alluvial terraces along tributary valleys. The high loess tablelands, which often had a broad and stable surface, were occupied by many prehistoric settlements. In addition, the edges of alluvial fans were also popular locations for prehistoric settlements due to their optimal soils and close to springs and groundwater. Because of these, some late-Yangshao to Longshan settlements moved to loess tablelands and alluvial fans (Wei and Zhang, 2017). The Longshan-period settlement changes in the Sanmenxia Gorge and Zhuding 铸鼎 *yuan* region shared similarities with those in Guanzhong, marked by an evident decline from the late-Yangshao period and subsequently by frequent movements between tableland tops and alluvial bottoms.

The archaeological records of Longshan-period occupation in both Guanzhong and Sanmenxia are obscure, especially compared to the corpus of the middle-and-late Yangshao data. Whilst this could be due to an imbalanced coverage of archaeological data, environmental aspects may have played a role. The acceleration of settlement construction and economic production on the Longshan-era Loess Plateau caused increasingly detrimental impact on the environment. At Xiaweiluo 下魏洛 in Xunyi many archaeological features are found situated on or close to fragmented landforms (Figure 13b). Standing in front of the massive ravine, one wonders about the cause and timeline of such severe erosion and whether the Longshan people had to live with it. Early proponents of the fertility of loess to agricultural production, such as Ho Pingti (1917–2012), did not consider this critical factor. Yan (2008) nonetheless noticed the importance of it and suggested that as fertile as the loess might have been for dryland farming, the fragmentation of the loess landscape might have prohibited the emergence of mega-sized regional centres during the Bronze Age. Although this 'environmental-deterministic' view requires a more rigorous scrutiny, the propensity for erosion on the loess highlands would certainly have impacted the socio-economic developments during the Longshan period and Bronze Age. The porous nature of loess has micro-scale and macro-scale social and environmental implications. The high porosity of loess allows it to retain capillary water and facilitate nutrient uptake of living creatures. On the other hand, the increasingly porous loess terrains might have restricted the growth of large regional centres whilst also opening up more transmission routes before the erosion reached a severe level (i.e., creation of massive, impenetrable gullies) and prevented communication even between neighbouring villagers.

In summary, different regions of the Longshan-period loess highlands were interwoven closely through multi-directional economic and cultural interactions, numerous transmission routes, and highly fluid socio-economic boundaries. The encounter between Shimao and Taosi might be spectacular and influential, but interactions between smaller social units such as cave-house settlements and through trade of salt and other products were likely just as prevalent and permeating. Not only were high-value objects such as jade and painted pottery and pioneering technologies including early bronze casting were shared, but there likely existed strong networks of goods circulation and population migration at different levels of local societies. As aforementioned, the Linfen Basin, for instance, received multiple influences from many neighbouring and far regions whilst its own cultural elements also spread widely (Zhang H., 2022). Similarly, the stone sculptures at Shimao suggest even wider connections between Shimao, the post-Shijiahe culture, Central Asia, and other regions (Sun and Shao, 2020). Additionally, salient characteristics of lives on the loss highlands were spread and transformed, such as the triple-legged *weng* jars and many greyish-coloured pottery sets, and cave houses and interior decoration techniques. These interactions played a crucial role in maintaining, altering, and reorganising agropastoral-agricultural boundaries, economic production zones, and other cultural spheres, making the highlands a major player to the rise of Chinese Civilisations.

4 The Lowlands

The lowlands primarily consist of alluvial lowlands in the Middle-and-Lower Yellow River and Middle-and-Lower Yangtze River regions and some of the intermediate zones between the highlands and lowlands. During the late Holocene, rice farming underwent an unprecedented intensification and became the foundation of regional civilisations along the Yangtze, whilst multi-cropping farming systems were also established in other regions. Parallel with this, regional cultures devoted significant efforts to control and mitigate floods. The interconnectedness between environment, water, and crops gave rise to diverse social organisations and cultural characteristics.

Longshan Societies in the Circum-Songshan Mountain Region: Expanding Agrarian Societies between the Highlands and Lowlands

The circum-Songshan 嵩山 Mountain region experiences typical geomorphological process seen in the loess highlands whilst also displaying characteristics unique to lowlands. The region's landforms gradually descend from the Songshan Mountains to a ring of low hills and tablelands (500–200 masl) before transitioning to lowlands, including the Luoyang Basin in the west, the western edge of the vast North China Plains in the east, and the Ying 颖 and Sha 沙 River valleys in the south. The Luoyang Basin (also called Yi-Luo Basin) contains plains, low loess hills and tablelands, and high mountains (Figure 18a–c). The basin is crisscrossed by a dense network of rivers, most of which merge in the eastern basin, as the Yi-Luo River, and flow into the Yellow River. The Holocene environment consisted of high loess tablelands and low alluvial plains. Most of the tablelands remained stable during the early-to-middle Holocene, as evidenced by the developed paleosols. But from ca. 5,000BP, surface sheetwash started to transport loose sediments from the tableland tops to gully bottoms. Meanwhile, many small ponds and seasonal wetlands were created under a humid climate suitable for rice farming (Rosen, 2008). The wetlands gradually vanished during the late-Holocene dry period (Sun and Xia, 2005).

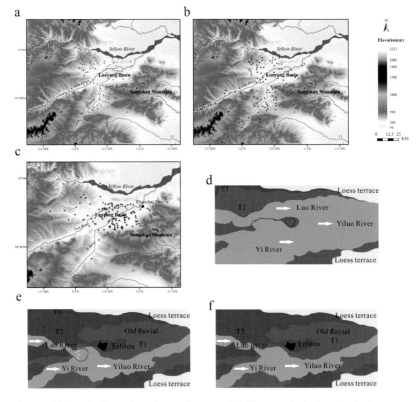

Figure 18 (a–c): Yangshao, Longshan, and Erlitou period sites in the Luoyang Basin, respectively. (d–f): Evolution of local landforms and water system at Erlitou from ca. 4,000BP to the Erlitou period, modified after IACASS (2014). T1 and T2 refer to first- and second-ordered alluvial terraces.

In the low-lying plains, multiple cycles of incision and aggradation created multiple-ordered alluvial terraces. Several terraces were already formed during the early Holocene, but were inundated periodically. By 7,000BP most terrace surfaces became stable, especially second-order terraces, which were ca. 10 m above the river water, facilitating large-scale regional occupation during the Yangshao and Longshan periods (Li and Zhang, 2020).

Building upon >200 Yangshao-period sites, mostly situated on tablelands and terraces, the region accommodated almost 300 sites during the Longshan period (Figure 18a–b). Whilst many of the higher-altitude sites continued to be occupied during this period, there was also a movement towards the lowlands as some large-sized sites were built on the flat and wide land between the hills and plains or close to the rivers. These Longshan-period settlements started to differentiate significantly in size. Several large-sized settlements (>30 ha) emerged as regional centres or sub-centres, surrounded by smaller sites, although their detailed structures remain unclear due to the lack of systematic excavations of large-sized settlements.

Evidence of Longshan-period animal husbandry in the basin is limited, but it is likely that domesticated pigs, dogs, and cattle were raised during this time. Millet farming played a dominant role in agricultural economies and soybeans were also cultivated at some sites (Chen et al., 2019). However, the most interesting change was about rice. Despite a decline in rice farming compared to the Yangshao period due to the drier climate and the reduction in arable fields, rice farming was still practised at some Longshan-period sites and even more Erlitou-period sites, including those on high tablelands (Li and Zhang, 2020). The high ubiquity of rice at sites such as Wanggedang 王圪垱 indicates that rice became popular among certain populations, which is also supported by bioarchaeological evidence (Chen X. L. et al., 2019). The adoption, and in some cases, revival of rice farming in late-prehistoric Luoyang Basin was related to the great relocation and adaptation of people to the low-lying areas with frequent floods and high groundwater table (Li and Zhang, 2020). These lowland residents grew rice and other crops, preparing for the 'great leap forward' at Erlitou 二里头 (ca. 3,800–3,500BP).

Records of region-wide floods during the late-Longshan period have been found in the Luoyang Basin (Zhang and Xia, 2011). The floods submerged the entire floodplains, low terraces and even parts of the high terraces. However, the rise of Erlitou greatly restored the detriment caused by the floods. Erlitou sat on a second-order terrace east of the confluence of the Yi and Luo rivers. The terrace transitioned gently to the lower first-order terrace without drastic topographic undulations. The rivers also formed large waterbodies encroaching the site (Figure 18d–f) (IACASS, 2014). On such vast and open lowlands, the site quickly expanded to >300 ha at its peak and became a super centre surrounded by >120 sites in the region, including sub-centres such as the Shaochai 稍柴 site (60 ha) on a transportation route in eastern basin (Xu, 2013) (Figure 18c). Abundant pebbles available directly from floodplains were used to build palatial stone beddings and produce different types of tools at Erlitou and other sites. The latter led to specialised production (Xu, 2013). Additionally, the burgeoning industries of turquoise production and bronze casting at Erlitou benefited from its uniquely advantageous location, which provided access to mines and other resources through long-distance exchange, contributing to a political economy that was central to the emergence and expansion of the Erlitou culture (Liu and Chen, 2000). Finally, the backbone of the state rested on its highly developed agriculture. Yields of millet farming were stable, and the contribution from rice continued to rise (estimates based on isotopic data suggest a ca. 20 per cent consumption of staple food from rice) (Zhang C., 2017). Soybean and wheat were also added. Similarly, its comprehensive inventory of domesticated animals includes mainly pigs, dogs, sheep, some goats, and cattle (Zhang C., 2017), which constituted > 90 per cent of identified faunal remains. Some animals such as goats and cattle might be brought into Erlitou from elsewhere, as revealed by their strontium values, in contrast to other sites where sheep and/ or goats were absent (IACASS, 2014: 1369). Change in food production was closely related to dietary revolution at Erlitou, best illustrated by new cooking and drinking vessels (Peng, 2013; Qin, 2019).

The fertile soil and sufficient water ensured agricultural success at Erlitou, whilst river floodplains and nearby vicinities provided raw materials for ceramic and stone industries. The flat terrains and rivers were convenient for trade and transportation. The surrounding low hills and tablelands served as buffering zones and provided abundant timber and many other essential and non-essential resources. The embryonic urban centre, growing population, resources that were pulled into it (sometimes considered an 'immigrant city') (Xu, 2013), and the rich repertoire of its urban and ritual life were new ethos that were not seen before and elsewhere. These unmatched environmental advantages turned Erlitou into a state-level entity in North China (Zhang C., 2007; Zhao, 2020).

Standing north of the Songshan Mountains, the northeastern Songshan region stretches out towards the low-lying plains in the east. The region's basal geomorphology includes uplands and lowlands that are divided by two tectonic lines. The mountains, loess hills, and tablelands constitute the uplands whilst the lowlands include alluvial terraces, plains, and sand dunes that are created by many rivers from the Yellow River and Huai River systems (Figure 19a). The dual loess-river elements also result in the distinctive 'platform plains' in the loess highlands. These plains (140–110 masl) have flat and broad surfaces that

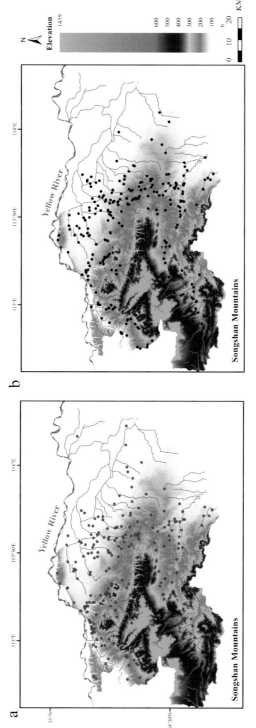

Figure 19 (a–b): Landforms and distributions of Yangshao (red dots in a) and Longshan-period (black dots in b) sites in the northeastern Songshan region, site data after Lu et al. (2021).

are demarcated by deep erosion gullies, some reaching 20 m in depth. Unlike either loess tablelands or alluvial plains, sediments in platform plains are dominated by loess, with embedded alluvial sediment lenses. Large-sized waterbodies sandwiched between the loess land formed during the protracted middle-Holocene alluvial aggradation. The lakes and wetlands on the highlands were drained as river downcutting resumed during the late Holocene, whilst the lowlands continued to be silted up. Most Neolithic sites were concentrated in the loess highlands, with only a handful being found on the edge of the lowland plains. Only after 4,000BP when most land in the plains became accessible did Bronze-Age settlements appear in these areas (Cheng, 2022; Lu et al., 2021).

In the southern Songshan Mountains, tributaries of the Ying River and a range of low hills and loess tablelands encircle many medium to small-sized basins. Like the Luoyang Basin, these rivers underwent aggradation during the middle Holocene, followed by a prolonged downcutting process (Wang H. et al., 2015). The latter gave rise to stable terrace surfaces with developed soils, upon which many Yangshao and Longshan settlements were located.

This highland-lowland dichotomy deeply influenced Longshan-period lives in the circum-Songshan region (Figure 19a–b). A three-tiered settlement structure was established during the Longshan period (Lu et al., 2021) but it also began to diverge in the late phase of this era. In Northeastern Songshan, although settlement numbers increased during this time, the regional settlement structure might have contracted to include only two tiers. This process, some called it a decentralisation, is different from the formation of multiple centres in the Ying River south of Songshan, including Wangchenggang 王城岗, Guchengzhai 古城寨, and Wadian 瓦店 (Cheng, 2022). These walled sites, although modest in scale, were surrounded by diverse landforms. Some were on the loess tablelands, some at the confluence of rivers, whereas others were even at risky places (e.g., close to floodplains of major rivers), reflecting a growing concern for water and other resources (Zhuang et al., 2023). The vicinity of Guchengzhai to rivers and wetlands resulted in an expanding enterprise on water management and infrastructure construction. Furthermore, important late-Yangshao developments (ca. 5,500–5,000BP) on earthen wall construction and other architectural innovations, as revealed in recent excavations at Shuanghuaishu 双槐树 and Dahecun 大河村, fostered more radical changes during the Longshan period. The walls at Guchengzhai, still standing 5–16.5 m high, and moats, 34–90 m wide and >4.5 m deep, would have necessitated substantial labour investment to construct and operate. The Wadian site also had massive moats, which were possibly connected to natural rivers when the height difference between the terrace surface, where it sat, and the river was much smaller than it is presently (Fang et al., 2018; Zhuang et al., 2017).

The Longshan farmers transformed diverse terrains into fertile grounds for reliable agricultural yields. Millet farming continued to prevail whereas rice occurred commonly at those sites equipped with water-management infrastructures such as Wadian (Liu et al., 2018). Some sites, such as Xinzhai 新砦, contained abundant rice (Deng and Qin, 2017). Soybeans were also grown and consumed, albeit infrequently. Domesticated pigs, dogs, sheep, and cattle were the main sources of animal food, occasionally supplemented with hunted deer (Guo R., 2020; Li, 2020). Despite the apparent agricultural continuity, dietary habits of Longshan people were changing. Isotopic evidence from Wadian and other contemporary sites reveals two different culinary traditions: a group mostly eating millet and very little meat versus another consuming abundant rice and meat (Zhou, 2017). The fact that they were buried in same places suggests the beginning of cultural integration, although such a process might be bumpy and conflict-prone. In the following Xinzhai-Erlitou period, multiple-ringed moats (e.g., Dongzhao 东赵) were built as the expanding settlements intensified their responses to water and other environmental problems on the lowlands. However, although experimentation on multi-cropping continued, millet remained predominant, with sophisticated field management, and rice only accounted for a minor proportion (Tang et al., 2018; Yang et al., 2017).

The Fen-Wei Basin and the circum-Songshan regions overlap substantially with the territory of the Central Plains region, which is widely considered the cradle of Chinese Civilisation. The region comprises heterogeneous landforms ranging across the highlands, lowlands, and those transitional zones. The close interactions between communities living on these diverse terrains created a powerful vector driving economic growth and social development. Furthermore, most of the loess landforms and river terraces in the region displayed remarkable stability (Zhang J. et al., 2019), despite claims that some high-altitude places were once flooded during the late Holocene. The often widespread and horizontally distributed middle-to-late Holocene soil sequences provide direct evidence for this ultra-stable surface where Yangshao, Longshan, and Bronze-Age communities lived, farmed, and interacted. Finally, the combination of a stable landscape, favourable hydrology and mild climate, and fertile, self-replenishing soils provided an instrumental environmental foundation that fostered the dryland-farming-based civilisation on the Central Plains.

The North China Plains: Places of Opportunities and Risks

One anticipates some picturesque landscapes on a train ride from Beijing to Wuhan but might instead be underwhelmed by the expansive, level terrain (50–10 masl) that is dominated by farmyards. As one of China's largest and most populous plains, the North China Plains covers an enormous area of >300,000 km^2, only rivaled in size by the Gangetic Plain. The plains are a masterpiece of tectonic subsidence and alluvial sedimentation. Some 500–700 m thick alluvial deposits have been deposited across the plains, and they are still growing.

The Lower Yellow River Plains: Places of Bustling Cultures

The boundary that separates the Middle and Lower Yellow River, near the Taohuayu 桃花峪 and Mengjin 孟津 (Figure 20a), also marks the transition from the second to third tier in China's topography. Here, the elevation descends dramatically from over 1,000 m to 300–100 masl. The velocity of the silt-laden river water slows down considerably, leading to the accelerating siltation of suspended sediments. The Yellow River becomes an aggrading and frequently migrating channel. The riverbed is elevated at an unprecedented rate, causing frequent channel avulsions. These propensities make the river a highly productive machine for building land. Like an umbrella, the Yellow River and its branches form the tube and ribs, whilst the alluvial plains and numerous alluvial fans make up the fabrics (Figure 20a–b). As it sweeps through the vast low-lying land on its majestic journey eastward, the river merges with numerous tributaries, and the floodplains are intersected by countless alluvial fans. Most of the fans slope and spread from mountain tops to alluvial lowlands, facing northeast and southeast. The fan sediments were deposited in multiple periods from the late Pleistocene to late Holocene, interweaving with mountains, plains and lakes, and accounting for one-third of the North China Plain (Ma et al., 2015).

Because of the highly mobile alluvial fans, the deposition history of the transgressive fan sediments is difficult to untangle, as the old and young alluvial fans are superimposed on top of each other. During the early-to-middle Holocene, the fan-head had moved closer to the Qin 沁 River, whilst the fan-front extended to present-day Hebei and Shandong provinces, covering a much wider region than the underlying one. This alluvial-fan development coincided with episodes of active alluvial aggradation, creating 20 m-thick silt-dominant fan bodies (Ma et al., 2015). Through the incremental advancement of the fan-head of a new fan atop the front of an old one, the land-building process moved rapidly eastward. By the middle-to-late Holocene, most of the major fans had formed and much of the Lower Yellow River plains had emerged. The land is divided into four geomorphological zones around key points in Zhengzhou, Lankao 兰考 (Figure 20a) and vast areas south of the contemporary and historical river channels, each containing diverse landforms (Ma et al., 2015).

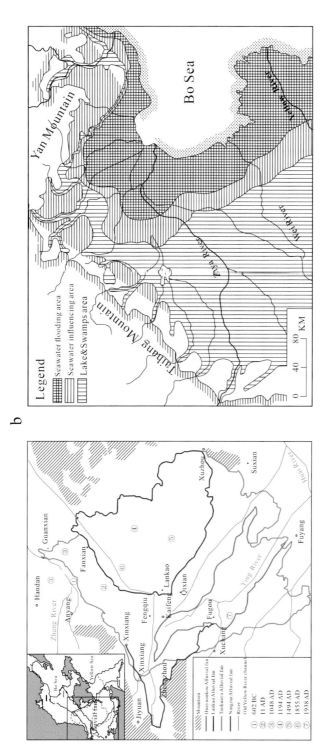

Figure 20 (a): Map showing main alluvial fans of the Lower Yellow River and North China Plain, modified after Ma et al., 2015. (b): Map showing major lakes and wetlands in the Lower Yellow River and North China Plain, modified after Wu (2008).

Of great significance are the high positions on abandoned floodplains and the sand dunes, and low hills where archaeological sites are often found.

Before the construction of large-scale dams and hydraulic infrastructures ca. 2,000 years ago, the hydrological regimes along the river remained untamed. The Yellow River was bifurcated by multiple branches, meandering through the floodplains and draining into lakes and wetlands. Channel migration exhibits a positive correlation with climate change, often occurring during the transitions between wet and dry spells in historic times (Wu, 1991). The river channels frequently avulse, flowing through north, south and east routes (Wang and Yang, 1993). Groundwater fluctuates at different depths due to varying sediment textures (Jia et al., 2002), adding to the complexity of surface-water conditions. Many large lakes existed across the plains (Figure 20b), many of which formed or continued to expand during the middle Holocene due to wet climate conditions, high sea-level, and stable alluvial condition (Wu, 2008). Whilst some lakes had silted up by the late Holocene, many small clusters of wetlands and lakes still existed between and in front of large alluvial fans (Wu, 2008: 311; Zou, 1993).

Two phenomena are worth highlighting. The first is the famous incident that the Yellow River once 'reaved' the Huai River channel in a local government's deliberate attempt to weaponise the river during a Southern-Song-Dynasty war (Han, 1999). The other is that the river became a 'suspended river' as the high sedimentation rate and relentless human effort to build levees and dams continued to elevate the channel above nearby floodplains. Both phenomena had far-reaching socio-political consequences. Prior to the historical era, most places in the Lower Yellow River would have been both tempting and hazardous for prehistoric communities. Tempting thanks to its lush environment with rich biomass and hazardous because of the constant threat of floods. Although thick alluvial sediments might obscure archaeological records and bias the spatiotemporal variations of archaeological sites, some distinctive distribution patterns of prehistorical settlements in the region have emerged from recent surveys (Li Z. X. et al., 2013; Shang et al., 2019).

In northwest Henan, the early Longshan period saw some communities began to explore Yellow River floodplains (Figure 21a–b) (Wang, 2011). By ca. 4,300–3,900BP, the number of middle-to-late Longshan sites rose to >130, mostly located along the Yellow River and its tributaries. The abandoned channels, crevasse splays, and remnant loess hills on natural levees proved to be attractive places, where large-sized walled settlements such as Xijincheng 西金城 are found. Thiessen polygon analysis shows that these walled sites were surrounded by smaller-sized settlements, which then formed site clusters, and that together they took up majority of the land suitable for farming and other

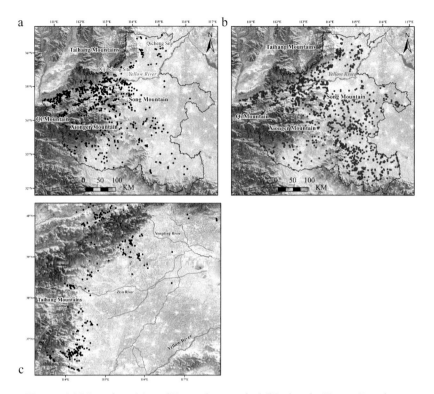

Figure 21 Yangshao (a) and Longshan-period (b) sites in Henan Province, including the northwestern Henan region. The purple dots show the exponential growth of Longshan settlements in the region, particularly the low-lying floodplains. After NCHA, 1991.
(c): Landforms and Neolithic sites in middle and southern Hebei, site data after Hosner et al. (2016).

economic activities. These clusters are thought to have formed diverse control and communication networks, which relied on rivers to transport and exploit various natural resources (Wang, 2011).

Whilst northwest Henan is partially shielded by low hills and loess table-lands, the middle-south Hebei Plain lacks natural elevations that protect it from the river. Neolithic sites were primarily situated along the eastern foothills of the Taihang 太行 Mountains to west of the Yellow River and around extensive wetlands, such as Baiyangdian 白洋淀. Vegetation and resources in these places were lush but the threat of flooding was also evident. Even during the middle-to-late Yangshao period, when there was a substantial influx of people into the lowlands, most sites were confined on higher grounds such as terraces or tableland tops. These sites subsequently experienced a decline during the late-Yangshao and early-Longshan periods when floods became even more frequent. As a result, the late-Longshan occupation of the region never reached the same level as before (Figure 21c). Alongside established agricultural activities, these Longshan communities also relied heavily on fishing and hunting as evidenced by fish bones and shells in faunal assemblages (Duan, 2008; Zhang et al., 2017).

Further to the east, *gudui* 崮堆 mounds, mostly of medium to small size, are a distinctive type of archaeological sites in the late-Holocene northeast Henan and western Shandong (Guo et al., 2013; Qin et al., 2022; Yu et al., 2020) (Figure 22a). Whilst some mounds stand 2–8 m higher than the current ground surface, many others, especially those situated near the palaeo-Yellow River channel, are buried under deep alluviums. The latter points to a fact that the living surface of these *gudui* mounds was substantially lower than the present-day one. As the regional groundwater rose during the late Holocene, most low-lying areas became submerged, and the Longshan people were compelled to retreat to low hills or sand dunes. They began transforming this new, seemingly unstable environment by building massive earthen walls and other public infrastructures at several walled sites such as Qicheng 戚城 and Jiaochangpu 教场铺 (Chen S. Y. et al., 2020; Yuan, 2012). Some of these sites were built directly on sand dunes, parts of which might be deliberately elevated or modified before the walls were erected (Sun, 2003), representing remarkable adaptation as settlements moved closer to rivers when the climate became more volatile (Chen S. Y. et al., 2020). Scholars have implicitly linked this development to the legendary tale of 'Great Yu's taming of the water' (Sun, 2003), which had profound social and environmental ramifications to society.

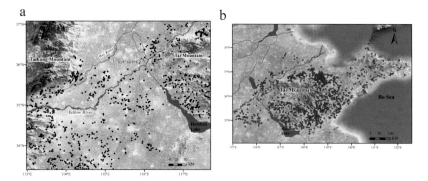

Figure 22 Landforms and Longshan-period sites in northeastern Henan and western Shandong (a), and middle and northern Shandong (b), in the Lower Yellow River, site data from Hosner et al. (2016).

At these *gudui* sites, above-ground houses were constructed on top of one another, inside which lime-plastered floors were applied and repaired repeatedly. Over time, these activities raised the ground level and turned them into more attractive places to live. The rewards of living in these lowland environments were high. As in Hebei, fishing was a crucial means of procuring food for local inhabitants. Agriculture benefited from the favourable hydrological and soil conditions, albeit with enormous risks too. Despite the excessive water surrounding them, these *gudui* residents relied heavily on deep wells for daily water needs (Chen, 2007). Mound-building and well-digging techniques enabled the occupants to survive and thrive in such flood-prone environments. Some of the *gudui* sites grew into regional centres, such as at Jingyanggang 景阳冈 (38 ha) (Li et al., 1997). The rammed-earthed walls were built by technology similar to that in the Central Plains, indicative of some regional interactions. There likely existed multiple transmission routes between the Central Plains and Shandong via these *gudui* mounds, representing Longshan-period riverine frontiers as climate became drier, and similar geographic units running parallel to them (Sun, 2013).

North and central Shandong played a pivotal role in socio-economic take-off during the Longshan period, following the profound changes in the late-Dawenkou culture (Luan, 2013). An astounding number of Longshan-period sites have been found on tablelands, alluvial plains and lowlands (Figure 22b) (Liu et al., 2021; Wagner et al., 2013). The density of Longshan occupation in some areas, such as the southeastern coastal region and the piedmonts of the central mountains area (Sun, 2013), reached a level that was not surpassed until the early imperial period (Fang et al., 2004). The northern plains area, in particular, saw a significant increase of Longshan-period sites, including those located in some of the lowest points (>5 masl), whilst the increase in other regions, such as along the central-Shandong mountains, was equally pronounced. From these areas rose some mega-centres (Zhao, 2011). One cluster of walled sites emerged in the southeastern coastal region, consisting of the Yaowangcheng 尧王城 and Liangchengzhen 两城镇 sites, each occupying one river valley and surrounded by some several hundred contemporary sites, including some medium-sized ones. Another cluster emerged along several river systems in northern Shandong, where each walled site seemed to focus on land and resource in one river and formed 'an economic corridor' between them (Fang et al., 2012; Luan, 2015; Sun, 2013).

The concurrent rise of these walled sites in different regions, as some have argued, was largely attributed to the economic prosperity brought about by fertile lands, skilled craftsmen, and convenient transportation (e.g., through rivers). Apart from the established millet farming, rice was cultivated in more places, where rice fields have also been found (Liu, 2022), and wheat farming gradually became relatively more popular among the Longshan farmers in Shandong. In regions like the southeast coastal region, rice was almost as important as millets (in terms of dry weight) in a mixed farming system and the consumption of it might have been related to social status change (Dong et al., 2021; Lanehart et al., 2011). It is also suggested that rice was cultivated at small sites and 'paid as tributes' to higher-ranking sites (Li, 2017). The role of rice farming in the formation of distinctive regional economies and its resilience in rapidly changing climate and social conditions warrant more scholarly attention. For instance, some have proposed that the change from wet-rice to dry-rice (unirrigated) farming in eastern Shandong from the early to late-Longshan period, as reflected in field-weed assemblages, might reflect a strategy to cope with potential water stress around the 4.2 kaBP event, in contrast to farmers in western Shandong who adhered to dryland (millet) farming (An et al., 2021). Domesticated pigs, dogs, cattle, and sheep were raised, although not every site had cattle and/or sheep. Comparatively, cattle showed a higher ubiquity than sheep, indicating different relationships between humans and these two 'new' species (Li, 2017; Sun, 2013). However, at some sites, including large ones like Yinjiacheng 尹家城, only wild hunted animals were found, whereas for other, fishing was a great supplement to meat consumption.

The highly-developed pottery industry of the Shandong Longshan culture produced some of the most refined objects in prehistoric China. Its signature eggshell-thin drinking goblets, for instance, required careful preparation of the clay, exceptional knowledge and skills on form shaping and decoration, and mastery of firing technique to produce. These specialised techniques were likely achieved through specialised organisation, which in return stimulated the production and social organisation (Sun, 2013: 451). Sun (2013) suggested that with these advantages grew a burgeoning 'middle-class' who played a key role in shaping regional economic structure, urbanisation, and long-distance trade. The distribution of the black ceramics, with their metal-like and futuristic styles, expanded beyond Shandong through trade routes that benefited from the convenient riverine routes that penetrated mountains and connected to plains and coasts. Environmental advantages, including fertile soils for agricultural production, rich resources for craft production, and convenient land-and-sea transportation, were key vehicles driving these developments.

The Huai River Plains: A Place of Large-Scale Gatherings

As a product of the mighty land-building force of the Huai River, the Huai River Plains might appear as vast and homogeneous expanse of flat terrains. However, in the headwater sections of the upper Huai River and its major tributaries, such as the Ying River, Sha River, and Ru 汝 River, terrains are dominated by low hills, tablelands, and alluvial terraces, which resulted from repeated alluvial aggradation and incision on remnant loess landforms during the Holocene.

Such topographic undulations gradually gave way to predominant alluvial aggradation once the rivers emerged from the mountain piedmonts. The rivers flowed into the Huai River from north and south, forming a dense river network resembling that of the Lower Yellow River (Figure 23). The Holocene Huai River channel had shifted southward, feeding into many tributaries and lakes (Jin, 1990). The middle-to-northern part of the plains is dominated by low-lying land (20–40 masl), leaning from northwest to southeast, where the tributaries join the main Huai River channel. Although these tributaries sometimes seem like trickling streams, they transported and deposited huge volumes of alluviums. Further downstream to the Huai River Delta, a considerable part is covered by the Yellow River Delta, and its Holocene sedimentation history receives little studies. From ca. 7,000BP, some south-north running ridges emerged and gradually widened on the furthermost west of the plain, fostering the formation of lagoons, reservoirs, and more ridges (Xu et al., 2011; Xu et al., 2010). By the

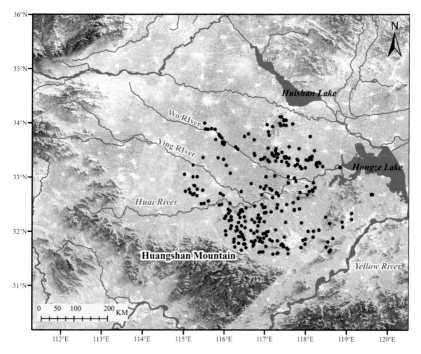

Figure 23 Landforms and Longshan-period sites in the Huai River valleys, site data from Hosner et al. (2016).

late Holocene, vast living space emerged in these extremely low-lying terrains. The region's monsoonal climate regime, with 60 per cent of the rainfall falling in summer months, causes frequent floods and droughts (Xu et al., 1994). The climate was becoming drier between ca. 5,000–4,000BP, and the vegetation was dominated by sparse coniferous-deciduous forest-grassland (Hu, 2019).

The peopling of the region accelerated from the Dawenkou to Longshan culture (5,500–4,300BP) (cf. Zhang, 2018), with the number of Longshan-period sites reaching hundreds (Figure 23). On the Eastern Henan Plains, Longshan-period sites were typically established on remnant tablelands and low terraces, which experienced periodic flooding. In the heartland of the Huai River Plain, whilst settlement development in its northern part might have stagnated during the Longshan period, an expansion had reached the southern hills and high-altitude areas (Hu, 2019; Zheng et al., 2018). The settlement number increased from ca. 50 to ca. 130 in Anhui, with more sites venturing into the southern region near the river and mountains as the climate became gradually drier, and previously flooded land emerged (Hu et al., 2018). Another significant development was the occupation of the deltaic lowlands. Whilst some late-Dawenkou-Liangzhu culture sites initially occurred in these areas, most were inundated and abandoned due to their low-lying position (0–3 masl), coinciding with some minor-scale sea-level fluctuations, before they reappeared during the middle-to-late Longshan period (4,300–4,000BP) (Wang and Chen, 2004; Xu et al., 2011). Occupying diverse terrains, the sites formed several clusters in the central Huai River Plains and along the main river (Huang et al., 2005). Most clusters consisted of small to medium-sized sites (1–10 ha) without evident differentiation (Xu, 2018).

However, some large regional centres had risen in places with good connections. The Yuhui 禹会 site, located right next to the Huai River, measures ca. 50 ha, with large-sized monuments and abundant artefacts (Luan, 2014). At other sites, earthen walls were erected on terraces and tablelands, mud-bricked houses were built in rows, and uniform spatial planning (e.g., central axis at Pingliangtai 平粮台) was maintained. It is striking that some walled sites such as Pingliangtai overlay directly on flood deposits, indicating that the construction took place immediately or not long after floods (Li et al., 2023). This prompted a series of innovations in water management. Moats and drainage ditches were dug, both inside and outside the settlements such as Haojiatai 郝家台 and Pingliangtai (Zhuang et al., 2023); and ceramic drainage pipes were invented and widely applied during construction and maintenance activities. This complete drainage system was essential in an environment that was fertile but prone to regular floods. Water had a profound impact on settlement planning and determined the rhythm of social and economic life at these sites. The spatial patterning of hydraulic infrastructures indicates that water management was a household and communal-based practice and that its development was parallel to other lines of dramatic socio-economic developments, some of which led to pronounced stratification (Li et al., 2010).

Despite having ample water, the Longshan farmers in the Eastern Henan Plain were relatively conservative in their agricultural practices. They stuck to dryland millet farming, with millet seeds accounting for ca. 90 per cent. They only cultivated a small proportion of soybeans and rice, although consumption of them might not be uncommon due to their high ubiquity (Hu H. Y. et al., 2022). In contrast, in the heartland of the Middle Huai River a multi-cropping system dominated by rice and millet farming was established by the late-Dawenkou period and further consolidated in the Longshan period (IACASS and BMAP, 2013; Yang et al., 2016). The Longshan people continued to fish and hunt but might have also raised more domesticated animals, such as pigs, to supplement their meat supplies (Xie and Zhang, 2013).

The super connectivity of the Huai River Plains brought about challenges as well as possibilities. The region facilitated some spectacular encounters in prehistory (e.g., that of the Dawenkou and Liangzhu cultures as seen at the Huating 花厅 site) (Nanjing Museum, 2003). Such interactions reached the climax during the Longshan period through several transmission routes, making it a key intermediate geographic and cultural zone (Sun, 2013). Although its association with the legendary Great Yu 禹 might never be ascertained, some unusual archaeological features at Yuhui such as altars and ditches full of 'sacrificial remains' suggest large-scale social gatherings, likely participated in by different groups, including some from far away. The mighty late-Neolithic cultures from the north assimilated with cultures from the east, south and west through many geographic corridors. Some of the groups such as those around the Chaohu 巢湖 Lake and in Lu'an City might have played a more important role than others due to their convenient transportation. The Wanjiang River (the Yangtze River in Anhui) became a centre of the centre that connected major rivers, mountains, and plains (Wang and Zhao, 2008).

The Upper Yangtze River: The Dawn of the Early Civilisation of Baodun and Its Contemporaries

The Chengdu Plain (average altitude 400–750 masl) is semi-enclosed by high and low mountains on its western flank (Figure 24a). These towering mountains transition to tablelands before giving way to alluvial fans that unfold like a scallop shell east–west. Several major fans are distributed from the north to south of the mountain fronts and form composite alluvial-fan plains with

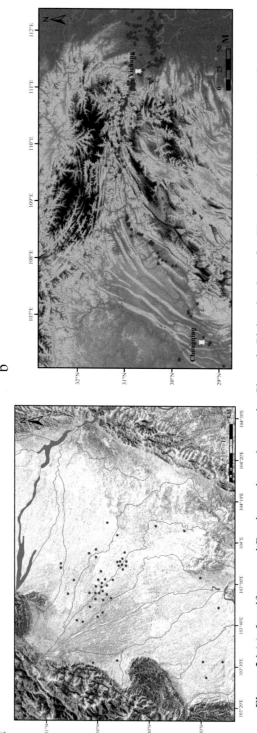

Figure 24 (a): Landforms and Baodun-culture sites on the Chengdu Plain, site data after Huang et al. (2017). (b): Landforms and Neolithic sites in the Three-Gorges region, site data from Hosner et al. (2017).

a 'dendritic drainage' system (Flad and Chen, 2013: 24). As one of the largest plains in Southwest China, the Chengdu Plain is fed by the Minjiang 岷江 and Tuojiang 沱江 rivers, which eventually flow into the Yangtze River. Once flowing out of the mountains, these rivers start to radiate out, supplying ample water across the plains but also creating torrential flash floods. On a temporal scale, the regional hydrology experienced a shift from being dominated by a dense network of rivers to including wetlands and oxbow lakes between 6,000–4,000BP. This coincided with some wet-dry climatic cycles, including a warm and humid phase between 7,500–6,000BP and a drying period from 6,000BP (Li et al., 2005; Huang et al., 2022). The latter caused vegetation to shift from a subtropical evergreen-deciduous forest with abundant ferns to a bushy-herbaceous dominant vegetation with sparse arboreal species. The evident decline of fern species indicates a substantial shrinkage of waterbodies. Whilst the pollen concentration remained low from ca 4,500BP onwards, the significant increase of gramineous pollen was attributed to increased agricultural activities. This also ushered in a trend of drastic change in vegetation due to regional and global climate events, such as the dry spells ca. 4,200–4,000BP, although the peak of the drying event might have occurred later in the Chengdu plain (Huang et al., 2022; Luo et al., 2008).

Following a sparse middle-Neolithic occupation, the Baodun 宝墩 culture (4,500–3,600BP) opened the prologue of the Upper Yangtze civilisation with the emergence of six to eight large-sized walled sites and some thirty-five smaller sites (He and Zuo, 2016; Huang et al., 2017; Jiang, 2015). Most of them are located on the fan-shaped plains with gentle terrains and hydrology at a time when many lakes were shrinking and more land were emerging. The walled sites, in particular, were situated on elongated tablelands parallel with the rivers and higher than the surrounding alluvial lowlands, a strategy critical for avoiding floods (Li et al., 2005). As a regional centre, the Baodun site was enclosed by multiple earthen walls with stone beddings and measured almost 280 ha (Fan, 2017). The site and its immediate surroundings were divided into variable tablelands, upon which wattle-and-daub houses were built (some reaching >200–300 m^2). A few other smaller-scale (ca. 10–40 ha) walled sites have been found (Flad, 2013). The Mangcheng 芒城 site had well-preserved architecture; and some features at the Gucheng 古城 site might have been used as altars. The rise of the Baodun culture coincided with a wave of migration from mountain fronts to alluvial lowlands and a profound change in the agricultural economies. Rice first occurred in ca. 4,600–4,500BP and subsequently overtook millets to become the predominant crop (Wan and Lei, 2013; Lv et al., 2021). Rice, coupled with sophisticated technologies for earthen construction and water control (He and Zuo, 2016), reawakened the long dormant fertile land. The level of rice production improved steadily as field management intensified and paddy fields expanded (d'Alpoim-Guedes et al., 2013), benefiting from sufficient water resources, fertile soils, and mild climate in the basin.

Despite the popular thesis that a widespread flood(s) wiped out the Baodun culture (Jia et al., 2017), geological evidence of such events is found only at a few sites where a 'hiatus layer' was sandwiched by the Baodun-culture layers (Jiang, 2015). However, at Baodun, the inner wall was wide and tall whilst the outer wall, which was built later, was narrow and short. Both the inner and outer moats were narrow and shallow. Excavations across the walls show no signs of floods. It is surmised that rice farming and earthwork techniques, both introduced from the east, enabled them to withstand precarious conditions and flourish on the lowlands (He and Zuo, 2016).

The Chengdu Basin is connected to the Three Gorges region through a series of ridges to its east. The Three Gorges consist of three adjacent narrow gorges located between the Upper and Middle Yangtze (Figure 24b). The famous poet Li Bai's lament about the 'hard road to Shu', which he likened to 'harder than scaling the blue sky' might apply to the Three Gorges region for its extremely heterogeneous topography. However, despite its seemingly impenetrable nature, the region played a key role in prehistoric regional interactions, especially the spread of rice from the Middle Yangtze to the Chengdu Basin. Archaeological sites were mostly confined on narrow terrace surfaces along the Yangtze and its major tributaries, as well as some wide valley slopes in the upper streams. They suffered from frequent flooding, as evidenced by multiple hiatus layers found at archaeological sites (Zhu et al., 2010). Nonetheless, the fact that Neolithic populations repeatedly returned to these locations is a testament to their remarkable resilience. The late Neolithic (5,000–4,000BP) occupation spread across the region, including some tributary valleys as seasonal floods receded and wide floodplains and terraces formed (Zhang et al., 2023; Zhao and Shui, 2008). The Daning 大宁 River valley has complicated terrains and turbulent currents, but it also creates one of the widest valleys, home to many Neolithic sites. Step by step, the early residents of the region overcame the challenging environment. They fished and hunted on the floodplains and mountains, and farmed on terraces, pushing forward frontier farmland into those previously inhospitable places. Some 200,000 pieces of animal bones were found in one single excavation trench at Zhongba 中坝 (5,000–2,200BP) with species from wide-ranging habitats and domesticated pigs and dogs (Flad, 2013). Interestingly, some communities might have developed a 'reverse adaptation' (Zhang et al., 2023) by deliberately focusing on fishing and hunting despite already possessing great knowledge of farming, or relying more on millet farming as rice cultivation would have required more effort in land clearance and water management (d'Alpoim-Guedes et al., 2013). These strategies clearly illustrate a great flexibility in the Neolithic occupation of the region.

Overall, the sites in the Three Gorges region were more densely clustered in the east than in the west, and tended to be on lower-altitude places than on higher grounds, with a few exceptions (Zhu et al., 2010). The region maintained some loose yet unbroken connectivity with its neighbouring areas through navigable waterways. These trans-regional connections are evidenced not only by the typological similarities in the artefact assemblages from the Three-Gorges and neighbouring regions (Flad, 2013) but also by distinctive inter-related economic structures. As early as the Daxi culture period, some riverine sites already engaged in long-distance exchange of stone axes and jade (Zhang, 2000). Subsequently, other goods such as salt were added to this pan-Yangtze exchange network. Zhongba, for example, was a specialised salt production site that thrived for almost 5,000 years (Flad, 2011), despite being disrupted by periodic floods (Zhu et al., 2005). The production and trade of salt, alongside other economic activities, significantly enhanced regional connectivity and stimulated the process of social differentiation (Guo, 2010; JMHP, 1999), shining first light of civilisation.

The Middle Yangtze River Plains: The Great Expansion of the Earthen-Walled Sites

The region encompasses the Jianghan basin lying to the north of the middle Yangtze River and the Dongting basin on the southern bank of the river (Figure 6), separated by the Huarong 华容 Uplift. Encircling the two plains are a range of high mountains; many low hills (>200 masl) are also scattered between the mountains and plains. About 70 per cent of its annual rainfall (1,400 mm) falls between April and September and inundates the surface. The region's main geomorphological types include high-alluvial plains (30–40 masl) situated in mountain fronts where the river enters the basin in the western area, low alluvial-lacustrine plains (<30 masl) in the central area, and low tablelands (with 1–2 m relative height) (Zhao and Mo, 2020). Its dense water network includes lakes and oxbow lakes, as well as the Yangtze River and its numerous tributaries. Initially a large depression with deeply incised valleys, the Dongting Lake became a large reservoir and gradually developed into a mega-sized lake with deep water during the early-to-middle Holocene. It is now China's largest interior lake, covering 18,780 km^2, fed by four major tributaries and many smaller branches before flowing into the Yangtze River (Lai et al., 2004). Between these crisscrossing waterbodies were alluvial plains.

After a stabilising river and lake hydrology between 7,000–5,500BP, the water gradually dropped from 5,500BP. One of the direct consequences was the shrinking lake with shallowing water. Land emerged and the lake was divided into smaller lakes. Whilst this hydrological regime was punctuated by oscillations, the contraction of lakes and dropping water levels coincided with a significant cultural development in the region. This was followed by another episode of substantial rise of river water after 4,000BP, accompanied by an expansion of lakes across the region (Shi et al., 2010).

In the Jianghan Plain, early human activities were limited to the mountain piedmonts in the northern and western parts, whilst most of the eastern part was devoid of human settlements. The emergence of the Qujialing 屈家岭 culture (ca. 5,100–4,500BP) marked a powerful expansion centred around the eastern Hanshui River of the northern Jianghan Plain (Shi et al., 2010) (Figure 25a). Its influence reached eastern Sichuan in the west, the Poyang lake region in the east, and most importantly, the southern part of the Central Plains (Zhang, 1992). The Qujialing site was situated on raised tablelands between the low-lying plain and the mountains, a desirable environment for the growing population who could build large-scale palaces and monuments and diversify their food production. Although the Qujialing people might have been exempt from the onerous task of building walls to stop floods, they might have already channelised the surrounding water for various purposes (Liu J. G. et al., 2019). At Yejiamiao 叶家庙, the late-Qujialing people began digging moats and constructing earthen walls as the site became an important centre in the northeastern Jianghan Plain. Similar evidence can be found at the Zoumaling 走马岭 walled site (Shan et al., 2021). These developments culminated with the emergence of the Shijiahe 石家河 walled site (Figure 26a). Measuring 180 ha, the site had earthen walls, moats and several ring-shaped mounds where social gathering and ritual activities took place and the deceased were buried (Guo, 2010). The cemeteries displayed signs of social differentiation, which was also exemplified by an emerging tiered system among the settlements in the region. These changes were sustained by a developed rice farming, supplemented by millet farming and other economic activities. Archaeobotanical evidence from Qujialing and Yejiamiao suggests that rice as the main staple food was established during the Youziling 油子岭 culture period (6,000–5,100BP) and further consolidated during the Qujialing period with sophisticated field management and food-processing techniques (Wu et al., 2010; Yang et al., 2020).

The Shijiahe culture period (ca. 4,500–4,200BP) witnessed the full-scale colonisation of the lowlands (Figure 25b) where intensified rice farming and enormous urban operations were achieved. The Shijiahe Site Complex now included some forty locations in its 8 km^2 territory, mostly on north–south

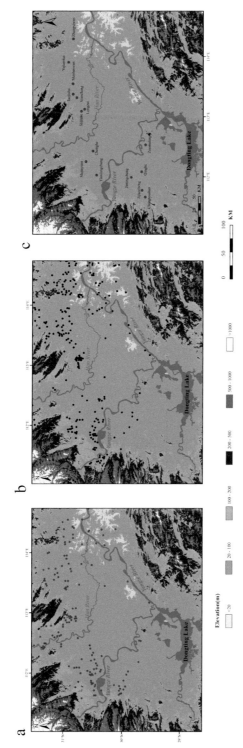

Figure 25 (a–b): Landforms and Qujialing (a) and Shijiahe- period (b) sites in the Jianghan and Dongting plains, site data after Hosner et al. (2016). (c): Neolithic walled sites in the Jinghan and Dongting plains, site data from Guo (2010).

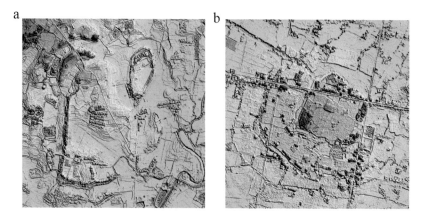

Figure 26 (a): Landform and layout of the Shijiahe walled site showing earthen walls, moats, and other features. (b): Landform and layout of the Jijiaocheng site system showing earthen walls and multiple ring moats. Both after Liu et al. (2019).

tablelands ranging in altitude from 27 to 200 m. A large hydraulic project might have been built according to recent surveys, possibly consisting of canals, dams, and small reservoirs running inside and outside the walls. This effectively transformed the sloping terrains and abundant wetlands into suitable living spaces and reliable rice fields (Liu, 2022), paving a solid economic foundation for the rise of Shijiahe as a powerful mega-centre that was occupied by 22,500–50,000 people (cf. Zhang, 2013) and with increasing social stratification. Among the functional areas at Shijiahe were the massive-scale craft production zones of pottery and other products, and ceremonial and offering zones which most conspicuously characterised the site. Shijiahe must have been attended by many people in the region and its products must have spread to places thousands of kilometres away (Guo, 2010: 254–258; Meng et al., 2017).

The Shijiahe culture's adaptation to the extremely resource-rich yet unstable environment was made possible by sophisticated landscape engineering, which became a region-wide phenomenon. The earthen-wall and hydraulic construction was imitated by many contemporary walled sites, each was surrounded by smaller sites (Figure 25c). Some focused on building earthen walls for flood prevention and other purposes, whilst others dug moats to control and harness excessive water, or redirected rivers for their own needs. As a result, the Jianghang Plain was now a more densely populated (Zhao and Mo, 2020; Zhu et al., 2007) and highly engineered landscape, a thriving hub where water was tamed and goods were exchanged, and a bustling place where social gatherings took place and ideas spread across great distances.

In the Liyang Plain of the northern Dongting Basin, most Qujialing sites were located on low tablelands along the edges of the lake. During the transition from the Youziling to Qujialing culture, the Chengtoushan 城头山 walled site (Guo 2010) gradually declined whilst the Jijiaocheng 鸡叫城 centre emerged. The latter was located on low-lying land, where a ring-moated settlement was established. By the Qujialing period, greater resources and labourers were pulled in to build the earthen walls. Many settlements mushroomed quickly outside the walls, forming a so-called 'Jijiaocheng Settlement System' (Figure 26b). This system became more complete during the Shijiahe period, consisting of earthen walls, multiple ring moats and numerous ditches crisscrossing the site and its precincts (Guo, 2010). Between the ditches were rice fields, sustaining a colossal scale rice farming (Fan et al., 2023). The interconnected ditches and moats successfully channelled water for irrigation, drainage and transportation, and converted Jijiaocheng into a land with great economic advantages for rice farming and regional communication (Guo, 2010).

The Shijiahe culture reached the northern piedmont of the Xuefeng 雪峰 mountain and as far west as the Wuling 武陵 Mountains (Deng et al., 2009). More sites occurred in high-alluvial land in the heartland of the Dongting Basin (Guo, 2010), whilst extremely low-lying places remained vacant of human impact. The settlement number grew exponentially from 63 during the Qujialing period to almost 200 during the Shijiahe period on the Liyang Plain. These sites formed a three-tiered structure and together they made the Dongting Plain a strong contender in regional competition.

The once prosperous Shijiahe culture might have experienced a sudden decline. During the so-called post-Shijiahe period (ca. 4,000BP), although jade and large buildings are found at some sites, most walled sites were abandoned and the settlement number dropped sharply. Thick alluviums covered the middle-to-late Shijiahe layers at some low-lying sites, indicating widespread floods that were caused by sea-level rise and hydrological instability. Although those situated on tablelands might have been protected from the floods, computational simulations demonstrate that those built on raised grounds would have been inundated (Liu J. G. et al., 2019; Zhao and Mo, 2020). Nonetheless, the causal relationship between the Shijiahe and post-Shijiahe culture and the floods should be investigated more rigorously using high-resolution environmental and chronological data (Wu, 2013).

The Circum-Taihu Lake and Yangtze Delta Region: Rice, Water, and the DNA of Lowland Civilisations

Situated on the lowest point of China's west-east leaning plate, the circum-Taihu Lake and Yangtze Delta region's exceptionally low-lying terrains

(2–4 masl) are extremely vulnerable to sea-level oscillations (Figure 27a). The relative sea level in the region reached a maximum level close to or higher than the present sea level between 7,000–6,500BP. This highstand persisted for several hundred years before starting to fall and rise again during the late Holocene (Zong, 2004). This hydrological history had a profound impact on regional geomorphology. Chenier ridges started to emerge and develop after 7,000BP, and became a natural barrier that blocked seawater transgression. The saltmarshes and lagoons on tidal flats gradually transformed into freshwater wetlands, paving the way to the formation of Taihu Lake (Zong et al., 2012). The palaeo-Taihu Lake was situated on a dish-shaped depression. The western lake was originally an estuarine environment, connected to the palaeo-Yangtze and Qiantang 钱塘 Rivers and dominated by brackish seawater until 5,000BP. After this, it became a freshwater lake and joined with the east lake, whose hydrological regime remained freshwater-dominated since 6,500BP (Liu, 1996). The lakes and surrounding wetlands created a typical aquatic landscape that dominated the region for the following millennia before the sea level rose again.

The proto-Hangzhou Bay funnel appeared from 7,000BP. Its full structure took shape between 5,000–4,500BP, effectively separating the Hangjiahu 杭嘉湖 and Ningshao plains (Wang et al., 2020). On the Hangjiahu Plain, the Holocene land-formation was dominated by continuous alluvial aggradation caused by high regional water table. Some land started to emerge from 7,000BP onwards and by ca. 5,500BP, the extent of land-formation reached the maximum. This land continued to be surrounded by wetlands, providing fertile soils and rich biomass for the Liangzhu occupation and its rapid expansion.

Some late-Majiabang culture sites capitalised on the improving environment and began building settlements on newly emerged land. During the Songze period, many more sites sprung up on the Hangjiahu Plain, especially on the southern sand ridges. The colonisation of the low-lying plains spread rapidly across the southeastern and southern circum-Taihu Lake region during the Liangzhu period. At least eight site clusters were established, which had one of the highest settlement densities in prehistoric China. Unlike the circum-Songshan Mountain region, where there is high settlement density across diverse landforms, the settlements in the circum-Taihu Lake region were predominantly situated on low-lying plains. This pattern represents a unique relationship between advanced architectural techniques, highly developed rice farming, and sophisticated social organisation that allowed for the mobilisation of large volumes of resources for the construction and maintenance of the Liangzhu City site and its enormous urban operation. The city covered ca. 300 ha and featured spectacular monumental architecture, including a gigantic

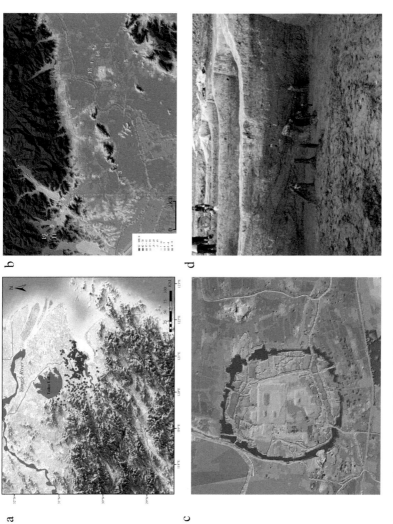

Figure 27 (a): Landforms in the Yangtze Delta and Taihu Lake region. Red dots are Liangzhu-culture sites in Zhejiang Province, site data from NCHA, 2009. (b): DEM photo of the Liangzhu City and its hydraulic system. (c): Water system in and surrounding the Liangzhu City. Blue lines are waterways and red areas refer to earthen walls. (d): Zhongjiagang canal. Photos courtesy of Mr. Minghui Chen.

palatial mound (30 ha) where many palaces stood, elite cemeteries built on artificial altars containing lavish goods, and numerous residential mounds and infrastructures, as well as extensive, multi-circled earthen walls (Figure 27b). The city was also protected by an enormous hydraulic enterprise, comprising high and low dams, and long levees with sophisticated structures (Liu et al., 2017). Liangzhu City is considered a proto-water city, which benefited not only from the hydraulic project but also from its water gates and canals used for transportation and other economic purposes (ZPICRA, 2019). It was surrounded by some 300 sites (Figure 27a), where diverse economic activities took place, forming burgeoning hinterlands. One of the celebrated phenomena of the Liangzhu urbanisation was its successful transformation of vast wetlands through mound construction, rice farming, and other specialised economic activities across its hinterlands (Qin and Fuller, 2019).

Excavations have brought to the light fascinating mound structures and rice fields from the Liangzhu culture. At Xiaodouli 小兜里, six to seven mounds were built during the late-Songze period and enlarged in the Liangzhu period. The elongated mounds aligned 10 metres apart from east to west, and on top of them were *ganlan* 干栏 styled stilted structures, surrounded by graves. This unique arrangement of mound-and-stilted buildings seemed to have become a common mode of living across the Liangzhu world. At Maoshan 茅山, the rice fields reached an unprecedented 8 ha. They were divided by roads and bunds, with single units reaching 1,000–2,000 m^2, and equipped with complete water-management facilities. By employing new farming techniques that involved tilling, frequent irrigation-drainage, and soil amendment, the Liangzhu farmers successfully converted the soil and water into valuable staple food of rice (Zhuang et al., 2014). The wetlands became a land of abundance. Plentiful rice and other foods were produced. Bamboo rafts and boats were loaded with foods as well as stones and timber. Canals and rivers were dredged (Figure 27c). Food and resources were shipped to the city and overflew the granaries. These strong economic developments guaranteed Liangzhu's prosperity for the next millennium.

The southern expansion of the Liangzhu culture to the Ningshao Plains was a milestone event. The region's several cycles of marine transgression and regression resulted in the deposition of alternative hiatus/natural layers and cultural layers. Around 5,000BP, the region became a coastal plain with abundant wetlands. By ca. 4,500BP, the light brackish water regime gave way to freshwater as most of the plain had emerged, although it was periodically flooded by seawater. The Liangzhu people seized the opportunity and spread rapidly across the coastal plain. They brought whole-scale change to their southern territory. Their pottery assemblages, for instance, were as elaborate as those found on the contemporary Hangjiahu Plain. Recent excavations at Shi'ao 施岙 reveal how the Liangzhu farmers maximised the potential of a small valley. The area was initially utilised during the Hemudu period but was abandoned due to sea-level rise. Liangzhu farmers expanded the valley into massive, highly productive fields (9 ha) that matched the same scale at Maoshan north of Hangzhou Bay.

The Liangzhu civilisation also experienced a mysterious decline and the environmental evidence for it seems to be more direct, thanks to high-resolution environmental records, than that for the Shijiahe case in the middle Yangtze River. Liangzhu sites covered by thick yellowish silt, deposited during floods, have been found across the region. Such widespread floods might be caused by abnormal rainfall, but given their exceptionally long duration, they were likely related to sea-level rise too (He et al., 2021). However, whilst the impact of the sea-level-induced floods and storms cannot be underestimated, the dramatic fall of the once-flourishing civilisation was, to some extent, of its own making. As essential as they had been, by the late-Liangzhu period, many canals in the Liangzhu City had become narrower, shallower, or even completely silted up, indicating a relaxation of canal dredging (Figure 27d). If this was happening on a regional scale, the society's ability to absorb excessive water would have been significantly hampered. The region-wide inundation of the low-lying rice fields would have been the last straw to devastate Liangzhu. Although it is now also believed that some Liangzhu communities retreated to higher-altitude places (such as the mountain valleys in southern Zhejiang), the loss of the farmlands would have also meant the rice-based civilisation could not be sustained.

Late-prehistoric communities across the Yellow River and Yangtze lowlands enjoyed optimal environmental opportunities. First, as water retreated and the climate became drier, more land emerged, providing key resources for settlement expansion and agricultural development. Second, convenient waterway transportation became crucial to heightened regional interactions. Through large-scale earthen construction and intensive rice farming, these communities were able to conquer the once-inhospitable lowlands and enjoy a long period of regional prosperity. The challenges they faced, however, were enormous. One was frequent flooding with increasing climate uncertainties. They responded to these challenges actively by inventing technologies and reforming fundamental social organisations to tackle water-related problems. These efforts seemed to be effective in controlling the water, some of which became deeply and saliently entrenched in society. However, almost all of the regional civilisations, Baodun, Shijiahe, and Liangzhu suffered, to varying degrees, a mysterious demise, which was triggered or exacerbated by environmental, especially water problems.

5 Coasts and Islands

The history of the Liangzhu culture can be extended to the coastal lowlands. Were the coastal lowlands in Zhejiang occupied during the late Neolithic, and did the Liangzhu people establish a connection with these coastal communities? Recent archaeological surveys and excavations have provided clues to both questions (see below). The coastal lowlands experienced dynamic environmental changes during the middle-to-late Holocene, and as a result, the coastal communities developed unique lifeways. Like modern seafarers, many of these communities were involved in long-distance cultural interactions within and between different coastal areas and inland regions.

The Circum-Bohai Sea Region: The Making of the Coastal Interaction Sphere

The region includes a range of bays and archipelagos (Figure 28a). Holocene sea-level changes were directly responsible for the evolution of diverse coastal terrains, including marine abrasion landforms such as bedrock cliffs, and more importantly, different depositional units such as terraces, sand bars, shores, offshore levees, beaches, and lagoons (Yang and Li, 2001: 147).

On the southern tip of the Liaodong peninsula lies the Liaodong Bay, where long and narrow plains meander along the coast and offshore there are numerous islands. Climate became warmer and more humid during the middle Holocene. Despite a reduced humidity during the late Holocene, deciduous broad-leaved trees and herbaceous species remained dominant (Liu, 2015: 46). The Holocene marine transgression reached its peak between 7,000–6,000BP, when the seawater reached as far as 10 km inland and flooded the entire delta plain. The seawater began to recede from 5,000BP, punctuated by minor-scale oscillations (Shi, 2006; Zhao et al., 1979). The coastal plains in the east experience ongoing erosion that has erased most Quaternary deposits, with marine deposits being dominant. The western region contains hilly terrains with thin but widespread Quaternary deposits and a narrow alluvial plain composed of blackish clay. Due to continuous tectonic subsidence, thick alluvial and lacustrine deposits are found in most of the middle bay region (also called the lower Liao River Plain), where marine sediments are preserved only on the coast (Fu, 1989). The formation of the Liaohe River delta, fed by several rivers, occurred in two main stages. The geomorphological condition transitioned from a lacustrine environment between 11,700–8,000BP to a marine-terrestrial inter-tidal zone between 8,000–3,000BP (Ma, 2014).

Parallel with the rise of the Hongshan 红山 culture in the West Liao River is the equally deep prehistoric culture sequence in the coastal area (e.g., Xu, 2019). The intensified human utilisation of the coastal resources in the region during the late

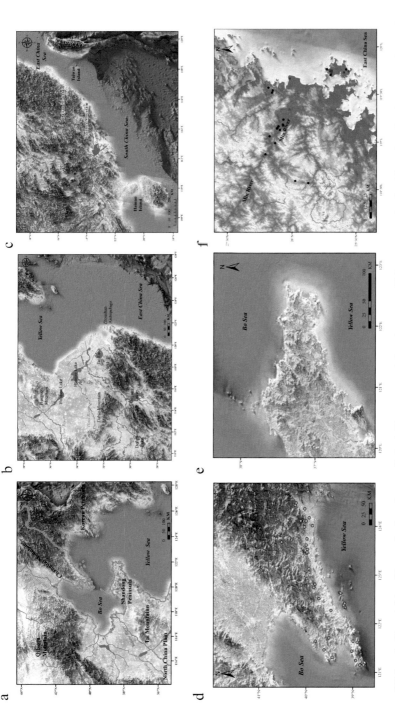

Figure 28 (a–c): Coastal landforms in the circum-Bohai, Eastern, and Southeastern China, respectively. (d): Xiaozhushan-III culture site in the Liaodong Bay, site data after Shi, 2005. (e): Longshan-period sites in the Jiaodong Peninsula, site data after Shi (2009). (f): Qiuketou (red dots) and Tanshishan (black dots) culture sites in Fujian, site data from TMFP (2017).

Holocene left abundant traces, the most important of which are shell midden sites on archipelagos and the coastal mainland. The long occupation deposits at the shell midden site of Xiaozhushan 小珠山 on Changhai 长海 Islands represent episodes of how these frontier communities received, reconciled, and transformed diverse economic, technological and cultural traditions. The Xiaozhushan-III culture (ca. 4,500–4,000BP) displayed significant influence from the southern Shandong Longshan culture (Wang, 2012), which arrived through a marine connection, whilst it also possessed some indigenous elements. The agricultural regime was dominated by millet farming, with additions of new cultivars such as rice, soybean and wheat (although some might not be cultivated locally) (Xu, 2019). The substantial increase in farming tools defied adverse soil conditions and terrains and created agricultural surpluses. This was greatly supplemented by one of the most developed fishing industries in prehistoric China (Xu, 2019) as well as hunting and raising domesticated animals.

The number of contemporary sites during the Xiaozhushan-III period on the peninsula increased to >50 (Figure 28d). In the south, shell midden sites continued to grow (Figure 29a), though with thinner deposits. In the north, some sites moved further inland and adopted new lifestyles (Shi, 2005). Other sites responded to a time of radical changes by maintaining some distinctive traditions such as building stone monuments. By occupying these diverse environments, the Xiaozhushan-III culture established a stronghold in regional interactions. They traded products of their own and from neighbouring cultures, including jade, but also perishable materials such as fur and leather to places far away (Xu, 2019). This paved the way for the formation of the so-called Northern Silk Roads in Bronze Age and historical periods (cf. Xu, 2019).

The rapid seawater advancement landward between 10,000–6,500BP in western Bohai Bay that caused the 0 masl contour to extend to 129 km inland was reversed after 6,500BP when sea-level rise slowed down and terrestrial sediment supply exceeded marine sedimentation. A cluster of small deltas was formed. However, there are shell ridges located several dozen km further inland (e.g., west of Tianjin City) which represent episodes of high sea level since 6,000BP (Liu, et al., 2015; Wang et al., 2020; Xue, 2009). The Holocene coastal landscape in the region overall was more unstable with higher-magnitude changes. Late-Neolithic cultural remains in this region are scanty, although this might be related to the lack of systematic archaeological surveys.

Moving south, the coastal landforms in Shandong Peninsula are dominated by low hills that undergo slow tectonic uplift and erosion, creating a meandering coastline (Figure 28a). The northern coast has a broad beach, the eastern coast includes the Yantai and Weihai bays, which are open bays protected by capes or small peninsulas, thus maintaining rocky coastlines, whilst the coast in the

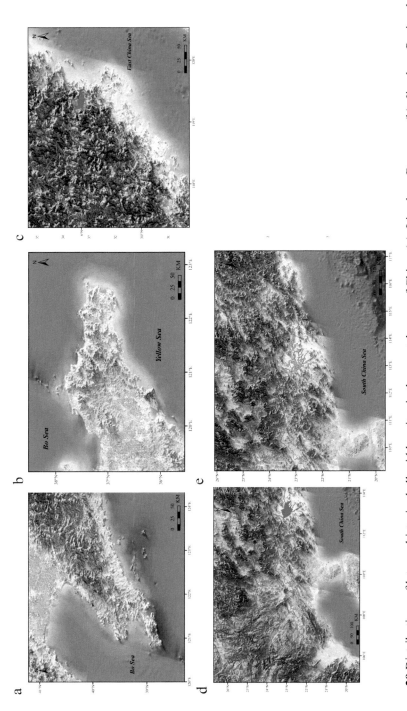

Figure 29 Distributions of late-prehistoric shell midden sites in the coastal areas of China. (a): Liaodong Bay area; (b): Jiaodong Peninsula; (c): Fujian coastal area; and (d–e): Guandong coastal area. Site data from Zhao (2014).

southern peninsula contains sandbars, lagoons, and gulfs (IACASS, 1999). Landscape in coastal areas changed from land, shallow sea, and lagoons to land again during the Holocene. The maximum marine transgression occurred ca. 6,000BP (Yang and Li, 2001: 156), best illustrated by the transgressive nature of the marine-terrestrial sediments. In the Laizhou Bay, by 6,000BP, the seawater reached ca. 7 km further inland than the current coastline and led to the formation of shell-rich shores and a winding coastline where the strait meets the bay. A massive sandbar emerged and effectively blocked tides from ca. 4,000BP when semi-closed lagoons were formed, with a considerably receding coastline. The lagoons and delta expanded during the late Holocene, forming a vast delta plain (Zhuang et al., 1987). Coasts from Penglai to Weihai and further east saw similar changes. Contrary to the above, coasts in southeastern Shandong are typical rocky-bay coasts. Coastal plains are rarely seen whilst lagoons are well developed. Because of this, the coastlines did not experience dramatic change during the Holocene, although in some estuary bays marine sediments can be found extending inland for 5–20 km. The optimal middle-Holocene climate in the peninsula supported a subtropical vegetation. This gradually gave way to forest-grassland dominated by conifer species from 5,000BP, with the presence of some xerophytic and halophytic vegetation (IACASS, 1999).

By 5,000BP, many sites, including shell middens, had appeared along the southern and northern Shandong coasts, as well as some archipelagos (Figure 29b). These sites were mostly situated on small tablelands, currently 20–30 msal, but they were much closer to the sea (an average of 3 km) when the coastline was higher (IACASS, 1999). Some sites were concentrated on the ⌐-shaped bay with abundant shellfish, although Wang Q. et al. (2014) also noted that some of the bays such as the ⌐-shaped Bay near Qingdao were intensively exploited by early prehistoric communities between 6,200–5,700BP before they were more or less abandoned. Nonetheless, the 3 km distance seemed optimal for the settlements to exploit marine resources. Life for these coastal residents was dramatically different from their inland neighbours. The architecture at most sites was quite rudimentary, in the form of small-to-medium-sized wind-proof semi-subterranean pits with simple postholes, some of which might be used seasonally (Shi, 2009). In contrast, remains of food production and consumption are abundant. A wide variety of shellfish, fish, wild animals, and domesticated pigs were consumed by the shell midden residents. Whilst isotopic evidence does not suggest they ate C4-based food such as millets, they might have obtained and consumed other plant foods through exchange with their neighbours (cf. Dong et al., 2020).

The close contact between these coastal populations and their farmer neighbours (Figure 28e) was facilitated by several factors. First, the economic differentiation between different regions of the peninsula created the need for regional exchange (see Section 4). Second, the coasts, the plains, and the mountains were all occupied, creating essential transportation routes. In particular, those situated along rivers in the middle mountainous areas were crucial points to connect communities on the northern and southern coasts (Shi, 2009: 91–96). Together, these factors established an advantage to further promote trans-regional interactions.

Scholars have suggested that the shell midden sites in Shandong had disappeared by ca. 4,500BP, caused not only by environmental reasons but also the colonisation of the Longshan farmers who brought in profound changes to the lifestyles of the coastal communities (IACASS, 1999; Wang Q. et al., 2014). However, the interaction between the coasts and the inlands did not cease entirely. Some coastal sites might have become specialised in salt production during the Longshan period and their products would have been supplied to other Longshan communities through regional exchange (Shi, 2009; Wang et al., 2006).

Eastern China Coasts and Islands: Rice Farmers, Fishers, and Their Neighbours

Coastlines in Jiangsu and northern Zhejiang in Eastern China (Figure 28b) are generally straight and lack meandering bays and rocky cliffs. They are strongly influenced by the land-building process of the Huai River and Yangtze Deltas, with the sedimentation process on most coastal areas similar to those on the delta plains (Xu et al., 2010; Zhu et al., 2016). The middle-to-late Holocene coastal landscapes were dominated by tidal and intertidal flats, chenier ridges, lagoons, and beaches. Sea-level history and its impact on Holocene environment in the Yangtze Delta and neighbouring regions are briefly reviewed in Sections 2 and 4. This section only covers those coastal and island processes in areas of coastal Eastern China outside the Huai River and Yangtze Deltas and outlines key episodes of late-Neolithic occupation.

The coastal areas in southern Zhejiang are characterised by low-altitude (2–3 masl) basins surrounded by mountains and connected to the sea. Following a complex hydrological and sedimentation history (Lv, 2022), from ca. 5,000BP, the receding seawater promoted the formation of peat layers, which are commonly found during archaeological excavations, and chenier ridges (Feng and Wang, 1986). The terrestrial sediments supply quickly filled up lagoons and bays. Whilst the coastlines were straightened, those rocky coasts remained mostly unchanged. The Liangzhu-period sites not only sprang up in the heartland of coastal plains but also settled in places close to the seafront. For example, the Yushan 鱼山 site is currently located 7.3 km away from the sea but was even closer during the Hemudu 河姆渡, Liangzhu and historical periods. However, living in the seafront came with risks. Due to its low-lying position (almost at 0 masl), a small sea-level rise would have inundated the site. But the more immediate threats were high tides and storms. Evidence of extreme weather events such as coastal storms ca. 4,500BP and their devastating impact on Liangzhu has been found at several coastal sites (Wang et al., 2018b).

Liangzhu-period occupation of other coastal environments was proven to be both volatile and resilient. The offshore islands and archipelagos underwent more complicated coastal processes due to their fragmented terrains and frequent tectonic activities than the mainland. In these islands, incised mountain valleys were filled up by marine sediments, whilst the rocky coasts formed typical marine erosive landforms. In contrast, the low-altitude plains and beaches received abundant marine sediments and continued to accrete. Even during the stabilising late-Holocene sea level, many parts of the islands remained inundated by shallow seawater (Chen J. B. et al., 2021). The main island of the Zhoushan archipelagos, for instance, has beaches and coasts that are protected from waves but with complex tidal channels. The beaches gradually develop seaward, up to 400–500 m in width. On the edges of the beaches are Neolithic and historical sites (Li et al., 2007).

Although artefact assemblages unearthed from the Liangzhu-period sites in these islands show a clear connection with mainland Liangzhu culture, they also possess some distinctive local characteristics, especially red-coloured pottery objects (Zhu Xuefei, personal communication). Many Liangzhu-period sites have thin occupational layers from seasonal occupation. Some of the sites formed small site clusters. The presence of farming tools suggests that they had adopted agriculture (Wang and Wang, 1983), but the basic economic structure was different from that of their mainland counterparts. The Daxie 大榭 site on Daxie Island between the mainland and the Zhoushan Archipelagos was specialised in salt production. The site area became a freshwater environment around 4,900BP, but the mudflats continued to receive brine-rich water through tidal creeks (Lei, 2017). The late-Liangzhu people settled here and engaged in hunting, fishing, gathering and perhaps farming ca. 4,900BP (Dong et al., 2020; Guo, S. 2020). By the end of the Liangzhu and Qianshanyang 钱山漾 period (4,400–4,200BP), the residents had built artificial mounds and applied air-drying, leaching and brine-boiling methods for 'industrial scale' salt production that lasted for several hundred years (Li et al., 2018; Zheng et al., 2023). Daxie represents another mode of Liangzhu-period occupation that is characterised by its large-scale, specialised economic production. They must have developed intensive exchange links with their contemporaries, through which salt was exported and other products were imported.

Southeast and South China Coasts and Islands: Spread, Resistance, and Reception of Rice Farming

The coastlines in Southeast and South China once again become winding and twisting, featuring many rocky shores and erosive cliffs. The region also has two large islands, Taiwan and Hainan, and numerous offshore archipelagos (Figure 28c). The largest rivers in the region are Minjiang 闽江 and Zhujiang 珠江 Rivers, which create medium-to-small-sized plains and deltas. The fragmented coastal landforms are dominated by low hills, tablelands, and small plains. The continuous rise of the Holocene sea level reached the maximum level during the late Holocene (ca. 5,000–4,000BP) when the seawater advanced 50 km further inland, punctuated by several short-term and small-scale fluctuations. Abundant marine sediments were deposited during these events of seawater transgression (Wang L. et al., 2022; Zhang et al., 2009; Zheng, 2000).

The Fuzhou Basin is a narrow depositional basin in the lower Minjiang River, presently protected by a mountain split from the estuarine process and tidal action. However, most of the basin was inundated ca. 5,500–5,000BP, transforming some hills in the basin into offshore islands with scattered archaeological sites (Rolett et al., 2011). The entire basin emerged when the sea level dropped to a significant level around 2,000BP. The Minjiang Delta is small in size yet has a composite structure consisting of small deltas sitting on shallow marine sediments. The sediment rate is low, the underlying tectonic and geomorphological processes are complicated, and most crucially, most parts of the delta are submerged. The delta was unsuitable for occupation during the Holocene, and even today, its complicated terrains often cause problems to navigation (Chen et al., 1998; Wang et al., 2000).

On Taiwan Island, the coastal areas, especially on the west side of the island, aggradated rapidly as the sea level continued to rise in the early Holocene, followed by seaward progradation after 6,000BP (Chen et al., 2004). These processes created broad plains that would have been suitable for prehistoric living. The eastern coast was, on the contrary, dominated by erosive cliffs with strong tides and hilly terrains. The modern terrains with sizeable plains and river terraces did not emerge until 3,500BP (Carson and Hung, 2018).

Zhujiang River contains the East, North and West rivers that flow into a faulty delta basin before entering the sea. As the largest delta basin in South China, the region consists of separate small deltas which join in the middle of the basin. A delta shoreline emerged around 6,800BP as the sea level stabilised. The rate of deltaic progradation varied between the three rivers and at different times. The rate reduced from 6,800 to 4,500BP to 4,500–2,000BP, probably due to a reduction in sediment supply in the basin. The deltaic shoreline reached 30 km seaward on the East River delta plain and 40 km on the North and West River delta plains. For much of the Holocene, the delta basin was a large estuarine environment with extensive freshwater wetlands and rich natural resources (Zong et al., 2009; 2013).

The peopling of these coastal environments is shrouded in uncertainty. The Neolithic sequences in Fujian and Taiwan started at some shell midden and coastal sites from ca. 6,000BP and 5,000BP, respectively. The onset of a 'Neolithic' in Guangdong and Guangxi can be traced back to earlier times (at least 7,000BP) with diverse traditions. The coastal occupation is represented by the Xiantouling 咸头岭 shell midden site (Li and Liu, 2007). These early-Neolithic horizons already established wide connections with their upland and inland neighbours such as the white pottery linked to the Middle Yangtze River region. Such a link was further intensified during the late Holocene, from which distinctive local cultures emerged in the coastal regions.

The Tanshishan 昙石山 site of the Tanshishan culture (4,800–4,300BP) was situated on a small tableland influenced by high tides. Around 20 Tanshishan culture sites have been found on similar terrains some 10 km apart and 20–25 m above the Minjiang Basin plain and nearby regions (Figure 28f) (TMFP, 2017). These sites are generally small (1–2 ha), with varying depths of occupation deposits. Permanent residential architecture is often absent, whilst many burials found at several key sites (Wang, 2015). The Tanshishan people might have continued to mobilise seasonally but returned to these sites for ceremonies and related purposes. They exploited freshwater and marine resources from the nearby tidal flats and hunted animals, including large mammals from the surrounding hills, using different toolkits and showing initial division in gender (Tian, 2002). The most significant development was the wider application of rice and possibly dryland (millet) farming (Wu et al., 2022) as the Tanshishan people moved towards the coastal highlands. The Tanshishan culture's dual aspect in subsistence strategies, exploring both marine and terrestrial foods, were mirrored in their interactions with their neighbours which were also through both marine and terrestrial routes. Through rivers, mountain valleys and coastal plains, they encountered Liangzhu and other contemporary cultures from southern Zhejiang, northern Fujian and eastern Guangdong. With seafaring, they established contact with contemporary residents in offshore islands, Taiwan and places further afield (Zhong, 2005, 2015). Dotted between Taiwan and the mainland are many shell midden sites with rich archaeological remains and a strong maritime tendency in subsistence economies (Wu et al., 2021) (Figure 29c). They were important bridges connecting Fujian and Taiwan. Some of the island shell midden sites produced stone tools which were circulated in the region (Zang and Hung, 2001; Wu et al., 2021).

Cross the strait, the late-Neolithic cultures in Taiwan are represented by the late Dabengkeng 大坌坑 (5,000–4,500BP) and Yuanshan 圓山 cultures (ca. 5,000/4,500–2,000BP). Sites began to appear on more locations, especially low-lying coastal plains, and sand dunes and low tablelands on offshore islands as well as mountainous valleys (Wu et al., 2021; Zang, 1999), with a larger size, more permanent residential features such as stone-walled houses, and thicker occupational layers. Some cultures, represented by their pottery assemblages with fine cord marks, are considered to be 'advanced farmers' who had adopted rice and millet farming whilst continuing to fish and hunt. The importance of farming gradually increased (Lin and Zhang, 1997; Li et al., 2016; Tsang et al., 2017). However, at other island sites, fishing and hunting remained the main sources of food. Between 5,000–4,000BP, prehistoric populations in Taiwan and offshore islands learned from encounters with neighbouring groups, and migrated and adapted to new environments. Some of their traditions such as tooth-extraction reveal their connections with the mainland (Han and He, 2002). Others such as millet-related rituals might reflect their own distinctive cultures (Xu, 2006).

Late-prehistoric coastal sites in Guangdong and Guangxi were mainly distributed in three zones: the Guangxi and western Guangdong region, the Zhujiang Delta region, and the eastern Guangdong region. The sites were numerous (Figures 29d–e) and had abundant cultural remains and above-ground and/or *ganlan* style stilted houses (Yang, 1985). In the Zhujiang Delta, these are represented by the Baojingwan 宝镜湾 (5,000–4,500BP) and Yonglang 涌浪 (4,500–4,000BP) cultures. The latter is characterised by pottery vessels with impressed geometric patterns (Chen, 2016: 82–84; Zhao, 1999), resembling those of the Haochuan 好川 culture in Zhejiang and the aforementioned Tanshishan culture in style. Hutoupu 虎头埔 culture (4,200–3,800BP) in eastern Guangdong (Wei, 2012) had a developed ceramic industry whose products might have spread to Fujian and Zhejiang. These cultures also had strong connections with the Shixia 石峡 culture (5,000–4,300BP) in northern Guangdong. To the west of the Zhujiang Delta, many archaeological sites have been found in the Beibuwan Bay and southern Guangxi. The artefact assemblages from these sites show great variability (Chen, 2016), including some with distinctive regional characteristics. For examples, the so-called Great Stone Spade remains (5,000–4,000BP), thought to be related to ceremonial activities, have been widely found around Nanning City (Li, 2011). The interactions between these cultures that shaped the diverse cultural affinities are much more complicated than can be explained here.

Subsistence economies of these late-Neolithic cultures were dominated by hunting and fishing (Chen, 2016: 150; GPICRA and ZMM, 2004: 353–360).

Gathered plant foods played a less important role. Scholars have suggested that these food production activities represented a pronounced shift from a hunting-fishing-gathering economy to a coastal-marine economy dominated by fishing (Zhang and Hong, 2008). Cultivation might have started in the Zhujiang Delta (Lǚ, 2007), but the picture of the development of rice farming is cloudy. This trend contrasts with the great acceleration of agricultural production further north in the uplands, and the reasons for these differences are much pondered (Zhang and Hong, 2009; Zhang et al., 2009).

The development of rice farming on the southeast and southern coasts was a prolonged process that was inherently constrained by land, terrains and hydrology in the region (Carson and Hung, 2018). The spread of rice farming might have started as early as 5,000BP, but only by 3,000BP did rice farming begin to spread rapidly in delta basins (Chen et al., 2023; Wu Y. et al., 2016), along the coasts and on the islands of the region, postdating the emergence of large and stable deltaic and coastal land (Ma et al., 2020; Rolett et al., 2012, 2022). Unlike the earlier farming experiments, which resembled dryland farming, late-Holocene rice farming was based on a developed irrigation system with paddy fields. Coincidentally, this was also when shell midden sites disappeared on the southeast and South China coasts (IACASS, 1997). It remains an interesting question to what extent the interaction between the rice farmers and shell midden residents shaped the cultural and farming landscapes in the region.

6 Conclusions

Introduction, adoption, and rejection of new cultivars and technologies were driving radical changes in the economic and cultural landscapes of prehistoric China and East Asia. Class differentiation and social inequality were growing as more surpluses were accumulated and competition for land and sources was running high (Wu et al., 2018). Territories were created, expanded and demolished whilst social and economic boundaries were pushed, negotiated and (re) defined. These great socio-economic movements took place in concert with changing environmental conditions.

Environmental Advantages and Economic Intensification

During the late Holocene, profound environmental changes occurred in various geological settings and were controlled by diverse allogenic and autogenic mechanisms on both continental and regional scales. Together, environmental changes created a powerful force that was instrumental to settlement growth, economic intensification, and frequent regional interactions. First, in the northwest inlands and northern steppes, the late-Holocene climate experienced an amelioration under the Westerlies system, creating conducive habitats for frontier agropastoralists, migrant farmers, and other actants involved in long-distance exchange which brought about extraordinary changes in farming and technological landscapes in the regions (Section 3) and paved the foundation for the transmission of bronze-casting techniques to the Central Plains. Second, despite the multi-millennia aridification, the loess highlands and neighbouring regions enjoyed a period of ultra-stability in land-surface condition during the late Holocene as geomorphological processes became less active. This stability made loess tablelands, platform-type plains, and alluvial terraces attractive places for the long-term growth and expansion of settlements, represented by the rise of Shimao, Taosi and their countless contemporaries, for example. Third, on the vast lowlands of the Lower Yellow, Middle Yangtze, and Lower Yangtze rivers, the late-Holocene environments were characterised by stabilising hydromorphic conditions under a weakened monsoonal intensity, which drained the wetlands and created abundant inhabitable land. This offered immense opportunities to rice farmers from Liangzhu, Shijihe, Baodun, and so forth, who, with advanced technologies in mound building and rice farming, could transform the once barren landscapes into prosperous rice-production systems and expanding urban centres. Finally, on the coastal lowlands, the receding seawater and formation of sand bars and chenier ridges provided crucial spaces where fishers, shell midden residents, and their farmer neighbours could farm, fish, encounter, and interact.

Late-prehistoric economic intensification and diversification underwent diverse forms and modes in different regions. First, the adoptions of agropastoral life differed in different frontier regions. On the Qinghai-Tibetan Plateau, raising animals adaptable to high-altitude and low-temperature conditions was indispensable to survive and colonise the high-altitude environments since growing crops and relying solely on farming were not always viable. In the southern Inner Mongolia, northern Jin-Shaan Plateau, and parts of the Hexi Corridor, water scarcity was a main constraint to agricultural growth, and communities shifted towards more drought-resistant agricultural regimes and agropastoralism as climate became drier. However, climate aridification occurred gradually, and hydrological conditions varied, with oases suitable for both farming and pastoral activities (Lu, 2014). Therefore, the adoption of agropastoralism might not be attributed to environmental change entirely but also as intentional choices or cultural preferences. Because of this, the agropastoral lifestyles were fluid, frequently shifting between agricultural and agropastoral regimes, and the agropastoral frontiers remained highly changeable. Only in those areas north of the 300 mm isohyet was farming abandoned completely (Zhuang and Storozum, in preparation).

Second, the intensification of rice farming benefited from the expansion of paddy fields in scale and sophisticated farming practices with clear examples from the Middle and Lower Yangtze rivers such as Maoshan and Shi'ao. But in other regions such as Luoyang and circum-Songshan regions, the development of rice farming might be influenced by both environmental and cultural reasons (Section 4). The scale of millet farming also increased in some areas, such as the Bicun site on the Loess Plateau, where plenty of arable lands were available. However, the development of dryland farming techniques remained unclear. In addition, even in the Middle Yangtze River, rice farming was supplemented by millet farming, which is different from the monoculture rice farming in the contemporary Lower Yangtze River, calling for the need to re-evaluate the relationship between farming, environment and society. Third, these different modes of agricultural intensification and diversification were closely related to different couplings of landscape engineering, settlement patterning, and means of local and regional interactions. For example, whilst water management posed acute and chronic challenges to communities across the Yellow and Yangtze River lowlands, solutions to transform wetlands and manage water varied significantly between regions. Different methods to build earthen walls, erect mounds, dig moats and channels, and construct ancillary hydraulic infrastructures, were employed from north to south and west to east of the lowlands. Equally, highland societies developed various techniques and cognitive landform choices to deal with water and land shortage, although the evidence is often indirect and ambiguous. It is argued that the environment-based economic diversity was related to the so-called primary civilisations such as Liangzhu and Shijiahe characterised by distinctive regional economic structures and their exploitation of local resources, which led to the accumulation of wealth. This is different from Taosi and Shimao on the highlands who emphasised new forms of social governance in a highly connected environment (e.g., Zhang H., 2022).

Interactions within and between Highlands, Lowlands, and Coastal Areas

The differences summarised above impacted settlement distributions and the making of the late-prehistoric highlands, lowlands, and coastal landscapes. The highland environments are more diverse than commonly appreciated. The low-altitude valleys on the Qinghai-Tibetan Plateau, the lake basins and riverine environments on the Loess Plateau, and the valley bottoms and oases are among those 'heterogeneous' components of the highland landscapes. Even in the Lower Yangtze River region with its predominantly low-lying terrains, there were 'high villages' and 'low villages' distributed on different terrains and organised through different structures during historical times (Lu, 2014). This pattern of settlement distribution was likely similar in the late-Neolithic lowlands, although more detailed studies are required. Similarly, the coastal areas had some of the most heterogeneous landforms and meandering coastlines. These variations in topography and economic structures triggered an unprecedented wave of intra-regional interactions. The agropastoralists, for example, would have migrated between different locations on seasonal and annual bases. Eleventh-century-AD records from Tibet showed that farming in river valleys constituted a crucial part of agropastoral life (Lu, 2014). Similarly, whilst the Longshan-period Shimao, Bicun, and their contemporaries built their ostentatious walled sites on loess tablelands and hills, they certainly must have explored the lower-altitude terraces and valley bottoms through intensive economic and other activities. Despite their predominant focus on the loess tablelands and terraces, Longshan communities across the highlands regions were closely interwoven with their neighbours, which profoundly defined the highland landscapes. On a similar vein, late-prehistoric lowland communities on different terrains would have been in close contacts with each other. A proper urban-rural division surrounding the Liangzhu City had emerged, for instance (Zhao, 2017); Shijiahe also maintained strong links with its neighbours.

Concomitant with these intra-regional communications were the intensified inter-regional interactions during the late-Neolithic period. The Hexi Corridor, the peripheries of the highlands, and the intermediate zones between the highlands and lowlands, such as western Henan Province between the Yuncheng Basin, Sanmenxia Gorge, and the cirum-Songshan region, created 'highways' for the direct and rapid connections between cultures living in high and low regions of the country. They acted as critical nodes that stitched together different regions, and fused their porous, swaying boundaries. Equally, the Yangtze River plains, the Huai River plains, and the East-China lowlands emerged as the most populous places where ideas met, populations converged, and conflicts occurred. Additionally, there were terrains that might seem difficult to overcome, such as the Three Gorges region, serpentine coastlines, and isolated islands, but late-prehistoric populations nonetheless embarked on frequent, long-distance contacts.

There were three main types of transportation and communication within and between regions in late-prehistoric China. First, on the loess highlands, late-prehistoric communities such as those at and surrounding Shimao, Bicun, Taosi, and their contemporaries, seemed to have primarily focused on the land-route communication, which allowed them to interact easily with their highland and lowland neighbours through the loess *yuan* surfaces and transitional landforms. This is fundamentally different from the classical centre-periphery and macro-regional economic structure proposed by G.W. Skinner (1925–2008) (Skinner, 1977), which considered riverine transportation an unparalleled advantage for important economic regions in late imperial China.

Second, in some riverine highlands, however, such as the Majiayao culture and its contemporaries in the He-Huang valleys, and most lowland territories, many of which were surrounded by natural waters, communication largely relied on water transportation. Those that formed alliances on infrastructural construction, such as building large mounds and hydraulic facilities, might be drawn closer, whilst connection between other settlements might be facilitated by various economic and cultural relationships (cf. Lu, 2014). Communities who can manage land and water, the two most important resources, and harness water transportation skills might gain an advantageous position. Third, late-prehistoric coastal and island residents were exposed and engaged in frequent communication and migration through seafaring, although the detailed information of this is often hard to pin down. One element that defined patterns of communication was the relationship between coastal residents and their neighbours. Whilst coastal residents on the Shandong Peninsula might form close economic relationships with their Longshan farmer neighbours, those on the eastern coasts might have had very different relationships with the Liangzhu farmers. Additionally, the southeast coasts were influenced by both marine and terrestrial communications. These interactions played a key role in further connecting prehistoric and historic China with East, Central and Southeast Asia, a more fascinating and complex story to be discussed on other occasions.

In summary, the highlands, lowlands, and coastal areas in late-prehistoric China differed significantly from those of historical and modern eras. A reconsideration of them should take into account the environmental and socio-economic diversity and diverse adaptations by different populations to the environment.

Environmental Challenges, Ecological Risks, and Social Resilience

Floods, droughts, erosion, soil degradation, and deforestation were amongst the emergent environmental crises facing late-prehistoric societies up and down the country. They occurred at either acute or chronic rhythm and required various approaches to tackle. Swift actions were imperative to mitigate the devastating impact of floods. However, without effective long-term solutions, the problem could recur. The severity of droughts and soil degradation could prove detrimental, but whether or not immediate actions were taken to address them might vary from one community to another. The negative consequences of deforestation and erosion might accumulate gradually until a threshold was reached, compelling society to take action. Overall, the frequency and magnitude of environmental problems differed across geographic regions, and strategies and solutions for these problems were contingent upon specific local and regional economic and governance structures.

On the highlands, anthropogenic impact on the environment was becoming evident. The prevalence of Longshan settlements on the loess highlands and increased earthwork construction and other economic activities, such as animal husbandry and craft production, placed growing pressure on the environment. Deforestation and surface erosion contributed to the fragmentation of the loess landscape. Abundant eroded sediments from the uplands were washed into the rivers and transported to the lowlands, resulting in a noticeable increase of sedimentation input and rate along the Yellow River catchments (Shi et al., 2002). As aforementioned, Taosi and other small-sized communities might have had to deal with surface erosion. In the short term, some of these problems might be turned into opportunities. For example, eroded sediments from upstream might become nutritious soils to land downstream. Nonetheless, erosion would have eventually caused severe land loss and become a detrimental factor for local communities in the long run.

On the other hand, these emerging challenges sparked innovative solutions. For instance, as one of the greatest architectural innovations ever seen on the loess highlands, cave houses represented a novel ecosystem and lifestyle in the increasingly fragmented loess environment. Cave houses diminished the need for timber, extensive land, and other resources during construction. Families related to such architectural units were often small, and sustained by small-scale dryland farming around erosive cliffs and grass-dominant land, although more evidence of water usage, farming regimes, and lifestyles is required to further illustrate the unprecedented adaptations of these highlands communities.

Late-prehistoric communities in the lowlands faced a larger-scale challenge, that is, to manage uneven distribution of water caused by climate change and hydrological fluctuations. Although some Longshan walled sites were located unprecedentedly near the Yellow River and its main tributaries, most settlements in the circum-Songshan and neighbouring regions were located on high terraces or tablelands. This was likely a strategic decision to mitigate the threat of flooding. However, as the climate became drier and more unpredictable towards the late-Longshan era, more walled sites, such as Guchengzhai, began to relocate to lower-altitude locations and build large moats and other water-management facilities. This entanglement between dwelling on low-lying land and the urgency to combat too much water can be more clearly seen among the walled sites in alluvial lowlands, represented by Jijiaocheng, Shijiahe, and Liangzhu, and their contemporaries (Section 3). These communities invested great economic and human resources to build and operate the hydraulic infrastructures. Water management became a pivotal fabric of their social and economic lives and defined the characteristics of social resilience and the process of social complexity in these new territories where they lived, thrived, but also struggled.

With water so intricately intertwined with late-prehistoric societies across China, it is also time to rethink some of the hypotheses on water and the collapse of societies. Take the issues surrounding the 4.2 kaBP event, commonly associated with dramatic socio-economic transformations in other regions (e.g., Weiss, 2017). A reduction in precipitation and surface runoff might result in more emergent land and therefore benefit the expansion of rice-based farming populations, providing buffering mechanisms such as hydraulic infrastructures were sufficient. Indeed, it has been recently proposed that a drier climate before 4.3 ka might have promoted the Shijiahe culture in the Middle Yangtze River (Wang et al., 2022). Rather than the simplistic propositions that the droughts or floods caused the toll of regional civilisations, a broader, cross-regional comparative perspective will be more helpful to understand how the climate change affected fluvial landscapes and societies.

References

Cited Chinese sources can be found here: https://discovery.ucl.ac.uk/id/eprint/10188476/ and www.cambridge.org/Yijie

Allen, C. F. R. (1891). *The Book of Chinese Poetry*. London: Kegan Paul, Trench, Trubner & Co.

An, J., Kirlesi, W., & Jin, G. (2021). Understanding the collapse of the Longshan culture (4400–3800 BP) and the 4.2 ka Event in the Haidai region of China: From an agricultural perspective. *Environmental Archaeology*, online version.

An, Z., Porter, S. C., Kutzbach, J. E. et al. (2000). Asynchronous Holocene optimum of the East Asian monsoon. *Quaternary Science Reviews*, 19(8), 743–762.

Carson, M. T., & Hung, H. C. (2018). Learning from paleo-landscapes: Defining the land-use systems of the ancient Malayo-Polynesian homeland. *Current Anthropology*, 59(6), 790–813.

Chen, F., Xu, Q., Chen, J. et al. (2015a). East Asian summer monsoon precipitation variability since the last deglaciation. *Scientific Reports*, 5(1), 1–11.

Chen, F. H., Dong, G. H., Zhang, D. J. et al. (2015b). Agriculture facilitated permanent human occupation of the Tibetan Plateau after 3600 BP. *Science*, 347(6219), 248–250.

Chen, F., Chen, J. & Huang, W. et al. (2019). Westerlies Asia and monsoonal Asia: Spatiotemporal differences in climate change and possible mechanisms on decadal to sub-orbital timescales. *Earth-Science Reviews*, 192, 337–354.

Chen, F., Yu, Z., Yang, M. et al. (2008). Holocene moisture evolution in arid central Asia and its out-of-phase relationship with Asian monsoon history. *Quaternary Science Reviews*, 27(3–4), 351–364.

Chen, F., Zhang, J., Liu, J. et al. (2020). Climate change, vegetation history, and landscape responses on the Tibetan Plateau during the Holocene: A comprehensive review. *Quaternary Science Reviews*, 243, 106444.

Chen, Q., Li, Z., Ma, Y., Zhou, Z., & Yang, X. (2023). Rice use history in Southeast China: Phytolith evidence from the Nanshan site in Fujian Province. *Science China Earth Sciences*, 66, 1108–1119.

Chen, W. S., Song, S. H., Wu, L. Q., Xu, H. D., & Yang, X. Q. (2004). Shoreline changes in the coastal plain of Taiwan since Last Glacial Epoch. *Journal of Archaeology and Anthropology*, 62, 40–55.

Chen, Y., Syvitski, J. P., Gao, S., Overeem, I., & Kettner, A. J. (2012). Socio-economic impacts on flooding: A 4000-year history of the Yellow River, China. *Ambio*, 41, 682–698.

d'Alpoim-Guedes, J., Jiang, M., He, K., Wu, X., & Jiang, Z. (2013). Site of Baodun yields earliest evidence for the spread of rice and foxtail millet agriculture to south-west China. *Antiquity*, 87(337), 758–771.

d'Alpoim-Guedes, J., & Aldenderfer, M. (2020). The archaeology of the Early Tibetan Plateau: New research on the initial peopling through the Early Bronze Age. *Journal of Archaeological Research*, 28(3), 339–392.

d'Alpoim-Guedes, J., Manning, S. W., & Bocinsky, R. K. (2016). A 5,500-year model of changing crop niches on the Tibetan Plateau. *Current Anthropology*, 57(4), 517–522.

Ding, L., Kapp, P., Cai, F. et al. (2022). Timing and mechanisms of Tibetan Plateau uplift. *Nature Reviews Earth & Environment*, 3(10), 652–667.

Dong, G., Du, L., Yang, L. et al. (2022). Dispersal of crop-livestock and geographical-temporal variation of subsistence along the Steppe and Silk Roads across Eurasia in prehistory. *Science China Earth Sciences*, 65(7), 1187–1210.

Dong, G., Jia, X., Elston, R. et al. (2013). Spatial and temporal variety of prehistoric human settlement and its influencing factors in the upper Yellow River valley, Qinghai Province, China. *Journal of Archaeological Science*, 40(5), 2538–2546.

Dong, G., Yang, Y., Liu, X. et al. (2018). Prehistoric trans-continental cultural exchange in the Hexi Corridor, northwest China. *The Holocene*, 28(4), 621–628.

Dong, J., Wang, Y., Cheng, H. et al. (2010). A high-resolution stalagmite record of the Holocene East Asian monsoon from Mt Shennongjia, central China. *The Holocene*, 20(2), 257–264.

Dong, Y. Chen, S., Ambrose, S.H., et al. (2021). Social and environmental factors influencing dietary choices among Dawenkou culture sites, late Neolithic China. *The Holocene*, 31(2), 271–284, online version.

Feng, Z. D., An, C. B., & Wang, H. B. (2006). Holocene climatic and environmental changes in the arid and semi-arid areas of China: A review. *The Holocene*, 16(1), 119–130.

Flad, R. (2013). The Sichuan Basin Neolithic, in Underhill, A. (ed.) *A Companion to Chinese Archaeology*, Oxford: Wiley-Blackwell, pp. 125–146.

Flad, R. (2008). Divination and power: A multiregional view of the development of oracle bone divination in early China. *Current Anthropology*, 49(3), 403–437.

Flad, R. (2011). *Salt Production and Social Hierarchy in Ancient China: An Archaeological Investigation of Specialization in China's Three Gorges*. Cambridge: Cambridge University Press.

Flad, R. (2018). Urbanism as technology in early China. *Archaeological Research in Asia*, 14, 121–134.

Flad, R. (2023). Long distance influences and local adoption: Technological changes in ritual and economy in late prehistoric Northwest China, in Hein, A., Flad, R. K., and Miller, B. (eds.) *Ritual and Economy in East Asia: Archaeological Perspectives*. Los Angeles: Cotsen Institute Press, UCLA, pp. 197–221.

Flad, R. K., & Chen, P. (2013). *Ancient Central China: Centers and Peripheries along the Yangzi River.* Cambridge: Cambridge University Press.

Frachetti, M. D. (2012). Multiregional emergence of mobile pastoralism and nonuniform institutional complexity across Eurasia. *Current Anthropology*, 53(1), 2–38.

Gao, Y., Yang, J., Ma, Z., Tong, Y., & Yang, X. (2021). New evidence from the Qugong site in the central Tibetan Plateau for the prehistoric Highland Silk Road. *The Holocene*, 31(2), 230–239.

He, K., Lu, H., Sun, G. et al. (2021). Multi-proxy evidence of environmental change related to collapse of the Liangzhu Culture in the Yangtze Delta, China. *Science China Earth Sciences*, 64(6), 890–905.

He, K., Lu, H., Jin, G. et al. (2022). Antipodal pattern of millet and rice demography in response to 4.2 ka climate event in China. *Quaternary Science Reviews*, 295, 107786.

He, N. (2013). The Longshan period site of Taosi in southern Shanxi Province, in Underhill, A. (ed.) *A Companion to Chinese Archaeology*, Oxford: Wiley-Blackwell, pp. 255–277.

Herzschuh, U., Tarasov, P., Wünnemann, B., & Hartmann, K. (2004). Holocene vegetation and climate of the Alashan Plateau, NW China, reconstructed from pollen data. *Palaeogeography, Palaeoclimatology, Palaeoecology*, 211 (1–2), 1–17.

Hosner, D., Wagner, M., Tarasov, P., Chen, X., & Leipe, C. (2016). Spatiotemporal distribution patterns of archaeological sites in China during the Neolithic and Bronze Age: An overview. *The Holocene*, 26, 1576–1593.

Hou, L., Gong, Y., Huo, D. et al. (2023). Isotope analysis for reconstructing the subsistence economy in Datong Basin, North China, during c. 4000 a BP. *Journal of Archaeological Science: Reports*, 50, 104065.

Hu, X., Lu, P., Li, Y. et al. (2023). Prehistoric damaging earthquake promoted the decline of 'Heluo Ancient State' in Early China. *Science China Earth Sciences*, 66, 1120–1132.

Huang, C. C., Pang, J., Zha, X. et al. (2012). Holocene palaeoflood events recorded by slackwater deposits along the lower Jinghe River valley, middle Yellow River basin, China. *Journal of Quaternary Science*, 27(5), 485–493.

Huang, C. C., Pang, J., Zhou, Y. et al. (2013). Palaeoenvironmental implications of the prehistorical catastrophes in relation to the Lajia Ruins within the Guanting Basin along the Upper Yellow River, China. *The Holocene*, 23(11), 1584–1595.

Jaang, L., Sun, Z., Shao, J., & Li, M. (2018). When peripheries were centres: A preliminary study of the Shimao-centred polity in the loess highland, China. *Antiquity*, 92(364), 1008–1022.

Jaffe, Y. Y., & Hein, A. (2021). Considering change with archaeological data: Reevaluating local variation in the role of the ~4.2 k BP event in Northwest China. *The Holocene*, 31(2), 169–182.

Ji, J., Shen, J., Balsam, W. et al. (2005). Asian monsoon oscillations in the northeastern Qinghai – Tibet Plateau since the late glacial as interpreted from visible reflectance of Qinghai Lake sediments. *Earth and Planetary Science Letters*, 233(1–2), 61–70.

Jia, T., Ma, C., Zhu, C. et al. (2017). Depositional evidence of palaeofloods during 4.0–3.6 ka BP at the Jinsha site, Chengdu Plain, China. *Quaternary International*, 440, 78–89.

Jiang, X., He, Y., Shen, C. C., Li, Z., & Lin, K. (2013). Replicated stalagmite-inferred centennial- to decadal-scale monsoon precipitation variability in southwest China since the mid Holocene. *The Holocene*, 23(6), 841–849.

Jones, M., Hunt, H., Lightfoot, E. et al. (2011). Food globalization in prehistory. *World Archaeology*, 43(4), 665–675.

Kohfeld, K. E., & Harrison, S. P. (2003). Glacial-interglacial changes in dust deposition on the Chinese Loess Plateau. *Quaternary Science Reviews*, 22 (18–19), 1859–1878.

Lander, B. (2021). *The King's Harvest: A Political Ecology of China from the First Farmers to the First Empire*. New Haven: Yale University Press.

Lanehart, R., Tykot, R., Underhill, A. et al. (2011). Dietary adaptation during the Longshan period in China: Stable isotope analyses at Liangchengzhen (southeastern Shandong). *Journal of Archaeological Science*, 38, 2171–2181.

Li, C., Cao, Y., Zhang, C. et al. (2023). Earliest ceramic drainage system and the formation of hydro-sociality in monsoonal East Asia. *Nature Water*, 1, 694–704.

Li, H., Sun, Y., Yang, Y. et al. (2022). Water and soil management strategies and the introduction of wheat and barley to northern China: An isotopic analysis of cultivation on the Loess Plateau. *Antiquity*, 96(390), 1478–1494.

Li, L., & Chen, X. C. (2003). *State Formation in Early China*. London: Bristol Bloomsbury Academic.

Li, L., Chen, X. C., & Li, B. P. (2007). Non-state crafts in the Early Chinese state: An archaeological view from the Chinese Hinterland. *Indo-Pacific Prehistory Association Bulletin*, 27, 93–102.

Li, Y., Shi, W., Aydin, A., Beroya-Eitner, M., & Gao, G. (2020). Loess genesis and worldwide distribution. *Earth-Science Reviews*, 201, 102947.

Lister, D. L., Jones, H., Oliveira, H. R. et al. (2018). Barley heads east: Genetic analyses reveal routes of spread through diverse Eurasian landscapes. *PloS one*, 13(7), e0196652.

Liu, B., Wang, N., Chen, M. et al. (2017). Earliest hydraulic enterprise in China, 5,100 years ago. *Proceedings of the National Academy of Sciences*, 114(52), 13637–13642.

Liu, L. & Chen, X. C. (2012). *The Archaeology of China: From the Late Paleolithic to the Early Bronze Age*. Cambridge: Cambridge University Press.

Liu, L., Shaodong, Z., & Xingcan, C. (2013). Production of ground stone tools at Taosi and Huizui, in Underhill, A. (ed.) *A Companion to Chinese Archaeology*, Oxford: Wiley-Blackwell, pp. 278–299.

Liu, S., Zou, C. H., Mao, L. J., Jia, X., & Mo, D. W. (2021). The spatial and temporal distribution of archaeological settlement sites in Shandong Province from the Paleolithic to Shang and Zhou periods and its relationship with hydrology and geomorphology. *Quaternary Research*, 41(5), 1394–1407.

Liu, X., Jones, P. J., Matuzeviciute, G. M. et al. (2019). From ecological opportunism to multi-cropping: Mapping food globalisation in prehistory. *Quaternary Science Reviews*, 206, 21–28.

Liu, X., Lightfoot, E., O'Connell, T. C. et al. (2014). From necessity to choice: Dietary revolutions in west China in the second millennium BC. *World Archaeology*, 46(5), 661–680.

Liu, Z., Wen, X., Brady, E. C. et al. (2014). Chinese cave records and the East Asia summer monsoon. *Quaternary Science Reviews*, 83, 115–128.

Lu, P., Lü, J., Zhuang, Y. et al. (2021). Evolution of Holocene alluvial landscapes in the northeastern Songshan Region, Central China: Chronology, models and socio-economic impact. *Catena*, 197, 104956.

Lu, P., Xu, J., Zhuang, Y. et al. (2022). Prolonged landscape stability sustained the continuous development of ancient civilizations in the Shuangji River valley of China's Central Plains. *Geomorphology*, 413, 108359.

Luan, F. S. (2013). The Dawenkou culture in the Lower Yellow River and Huai River Basin areas, in Underhill, A. (ed.) *A Companion to Chinese Archaeology*, Oxford: Wiley-Blackwell, pp. 411–434.

Lyu, Y., Tong, C., Saito, Y., Meadows, M. E., & Wang, Z. (2021). Early to mid-Holocene sedimentary evolution on the southeastern coast of Hangzhou Bay, East China, in response to sea-level change. *Marine Geology*, 442, 106655.

Lü, J., Mo, D., Zhuang, Y., et al. (2019). Holocene geomorphic evolution and settlement distribution patterns in the mid-lower Fen River basins, China. *Quaternary international*, 521, 16–24.

Ma, M., Dong, G., Jia, X. et al. (2016). Dietary shift after 3600 cal yr BP and its influencing factors in northwestern China: Evidence from stable isotopes. *Quaternary Science Reviews*, 145, 57–70.

Ma, T., Rolett, B. V., Zheng, Z., & Zong, Y. (2020). Holocene coastal evolution preceded the expansion of paddy field rice farming. *Proceedings of the National Academy of Sciences*, 117(39), 24138–24143.

He, N. (2013). The Longshan period site of Taosi in southern Shanxi Province, in Underhill A. (ed.) *A Companion to Chinese Archaeology*. Oxford: Wiley-Blackwell, pp. 255–277.

Owlett, T. E., Hu, S., Sun, Z., & Shao, J. (2018). Food between the country and the city: The politics of food production at Shimao and Zhaimaoliang in the Ordos Region, northern China. *Archaeological Research in Asia*, 14, 46–60.

Peng, J., Chen, S., & Dong, P. (2010). Temporal variation of sediment load in the Yellow River basin, China, and its impacts on the lower reaches and the river delta. *Catena*, 83(2–3), 135–147.

Porter, S. C. (2001). Chinese loess record of monsoon climate during the last glacial – interglacial cycle. *Earth-Science Reviews*, 54(1–3), 115–128.

Qin, L., & Fuller, D. Q. (2019). Why rice farmers don't sail: Coastal subsistence traditions and maritime trends in early China, in Wu, C. M. and Rolett, B. V. (eds.) *Prehistoric Maritime Cultures and Seafaring in East Asia*, 159–191.

Qin, Z., Storozum, M. J., Liu, H., & Kidder, T. R. (2022). Holocene landscape evolution in northern Henan Province and its implications for archaeological surveys. *Geoarchaeology*, 38(3) 320–334.

Rawson, J. (2023). *Life and Afterlife in Ancient China*. Dublin: Allen Lane.

Rolett, B. V. (2012). Late Holocene evolution of the Fuzhou Basin (Fujian, China) and the spread of rice farming. *Climates, Landscapes, and Civilizations*, 198, 137–144.

Rolett, B. V., Zheng, Z., & Yue, Y. (2011). Holocene sea-level change and the emergence of Neolithic seafaring in the Fuzhou Basin (Fujian, China). *Quaternary Science Reviews*, 30(7–8), 788–797.

Rosen, A. M. (2008). The impact of environmental change and human land use on alluvial valleys in the Loess Plateau of China during the Middle Holocene. *Geomorphology*, 101(1–2), 298–307.

Shan, S., He, L., Yao, S. et al. (2021). The emergence of walled towns in prehistoric middle Yangtze River valley: Excavations at the Zoumaling site. *Archaeological Research in Asia*, 26, 100285.

Shelach-Lavi, G. (2015). *The Archaeology of Early China: From Prehistory to the Han Dynasty*. Cambridge: Cambridge University Press.

Sheng, P., Shang, X., Zhou, X. et al. (2021). Feeding Shimao: Archaeobotanical and Isotopic Investigation into Early Urbanism (4200–3000 BP) on the Northern Loess Plateau, China. *Environmental Archaeology*, 1–15.

Shi, C., Dian, Z., & You, L. (2002). Changes in sediment yield of the Yellow River basin of China during the Holocene. *Geomorphology*, 46(3–4), 267–283.

Shi, Y., Shen, Y., Kang, E. et al. (2007). Recent and future climate change in northwest China. *Climatic Change*, 80, 379–393.

Skinner, G. W. & Baker, H. D. R. (1977). *The City in Late Imperial China*. Redwood City: Stanford University Press.

Song, J., Gao, Y., Tang, L. et al. (2021). Farming and multi-resource subsistence in the third and second millennium BC: Archaeobotanical evidence from Karuo. *Archaeological and Anthropological Sciences*, 13, 1–16.

Stevens, C. J., Murphy, C., Roberts, R. et al. (2016). Between China and South Asia: A Middle Asian corridor of crop dispersal and agricultural innovation in the Bronze Age. *The Holocene*, 26(10), 1541–1555.

Storozum, M., Zhuang, Y., Wang, H., & Mo, D. (2023). Geoarchaeology in China: Progress, trends, and perspectives. *Geoarchaeology*, 38(3), 263–267.

Sun, B. (2013). The Longshan culture of Shandong, in Underhill, A. (ed.) *A Companion to Chinese Archaeology*. Oxford: Wiley-Blackwell, pp. 435–458.

Sun, Q., Zhou, J., Shen, J. et al. (2006). Environmental characteristics of Mid-Holocene recorded by lacustrine sediments from Lake Daihai, north environment sensitive zone, China. *Science in China Series D: Earth Sciences*, 49, 968–981.

Sun, Y., Zhang, S., & Xu, Q. (2022). Pollen-based land cover changes reveal temporal and spatial differences of human activity in north-central China during the Holocene. *Catena*, 219, 106620.

Sun, Z., Shao, J., Liu, L. et al. (2018). The first Neolithic urban center on China's north Loess Plateau: The rise and fall of Shimao. *Archaeological Research in Asia*, 14, 33–45.

Tardif, D., Fluteau, F., Donnadieu, Y. et al. (2020). The origin of Asian monsoons: A modelling perspective. *Climate of the Past*, 16(3), 847–865.

Toor, A. (2013). Why did 28,000 rivers in China suddenly disappear?. *The Verge*, 3 April.

Tsang, C. H., Li, K. T., Hsu, T. F. et al. (2017). Broomcorn and foxtail millet were cultivated in Taiwan about 5000 years ago. *Botanical studies*, 58, 1–10.

Wagner, M., Tarasov, P., Hosner, D. (2013). Mapping of the spatial and temporal distribution of archaeological sites of northern China during the Neolithic and Bronze Age. *Quaternary International*, 290, 344–357.

Wang, F., Zong, Y., Mauz, B. et al. (2020). Holocene sea-level change on the west coast Bohai Bay, China. *Earth Surface Dynamics Discussions*, 8, 679–693.

Wang, H., Huang, C. C., Pang, J. et al. (2021a). Catastrophic flashflood and mudflow events in the pre-historical Lajia Ruins at the northeast margin of the Chinese Tibetan Plateau. *Quaternary Science Reviews*, 251, 106737.

Wang, S., Fu, B., Piao, S. et al. (2016). Reduced sediment transport in the Yellow River due to anthropogenic changes. *Nature Geoscience*, 9(1), 38–41.

Wang, S., Ge, J., Kilbourne, K. H., & Wang, Z. (2020). Numerical simulation of mid-Holocene tidal regime and storm-tide inundation in the south Yangtze coastal plain, East China. *Marine Geology*, 423, 106134.

Wang, T., Li, D., Cheng, X. et al. (2022). Hydroclimatic changes in south-central China during the 4.2 ka event and their potential impacts on the development of Neolithic culture. *Quaternary Research*, 109, 39–52.

Wang, X., Xiao, J., Cui, L., & Ding, Z. (2013). Holocene changes in fire frequency in the Daihai Lake region (north-central China): Indications and implications for an important role of human activity. *Quaternary Science Reviews*, 59, 18–29.

Wang, Y., Cheng, H., Edwards, R. L. et al. (2005). The Holocene Asian monsoon: Links to solar changes and North Atlantic climate. *Science*, 308-(5723), 854–857.

Wang, Y., Gao, Y., Zhang, Z. et al. (2023). Human–animal–environment dynamics and formation of pastoralism in the southern Tibetan Plateau during the Middle – Late Holocene. *Quaternary Research*, 114, 30–51.

Wang, Y., Liu, X., & Herzschuh, U. (2010). Asynchronous evolution of the Indian and East Asian Summer Monsoon indicated by Holocene moisture patterns in monsoonal central Asia. *Earth-Science Reviews*, 103(3–4), 135–153.

Wang, Z., Saito, Y., Zhan, Q. et al. (2018a). Three-dimensional evolution of the Yangtze River mouth, China during the Holocene: Impacts of sea level, climate and human activity. *Earth-Science Reviews*, 185, 938–955.

Wang, Z., Ryves, D. B., Lei, S. et al. (2018b). Middle Holocene marine flooding and human response in the south Yangtze coastal plain, East China. *Quaternary Science Reviews*, 187, 80–93.

Weiss, H. (2022). The East Asian summer monsoon, the Indian summer monsoon, and the midlatitude westerlies at 4.2 ka BP. *Proceedings of the National Academy of Sciences*, 119(20), e2200796119.

Weiss, H. (Ed.). (2017). *Megadrought and Collapse: From Early Agriculture to Angkor.* Oxford: Oxford University Press.

Wu, Q., Zhao, Z., Liu, L. et al. (2016). Outburst flood at 1920 BEC supports historicity of China's great flood and the Xia Dynasty. *Science*, 353, 579–582.

Wu, Y., Mao, L., Wang, C., Zhang, J., & Zhao, Z. (2016). Phytolith evidence suggests early domesticated rice since 5600 cal a BP on Hainan Island of South China. *Quaternary International*, 426(28), 120–125.

Wu, W., Zheng, H., Hou, M., & Ge, Q. (2018). The 5.5 cal ka BP climate event, population growth, circumscription and the emergence of the earliest complex societies in China. *Science China Earth Sciences*, 61, 134–148.

Xiao, J., Xu, Q., Nakamura, T. et al. (2004). Holocene vegetation variation in the Daihai Lake region of north-central China: A direct indication of the Asian monsoon climatic history. *Quaternary Science Reviews*, 23(14–15), 1669–1679.

Xu, H. (2013). The Erlitou culture, in Underhill, A. (ed.) *A Companion to Chinese Archaeology.* Oxford: Wiley-Blackwell, pp. 300–322.

Xu, Q., Xiao, J., Li, Y., Tian, F., & Nakagawa, T. (2010). Pollen-based quantitative reconstruction of Holocene climate changes in the Daihai Lake area, Inner Mongolia, China. *Journal of Climate*, 23(11), 2856–2868.

Yu, S., Hou, Z., Chen, X. et al. (2020). Extreme flooding of the lower Yellow River near the Northgrippian-Meghalayan boundary: Evidence from the Shilipu archaeological site in southwestern Shandong Province, China. *Geomorphology*, 350, 106878.

Zhang, C. (2013). The Qujialing–Shijiahe culture in the Middle Yangzi river valley, in Underhill, A. (ed.) *A Companion to Chinese Archaeology*, Oxford: Wiley-Blackwell, pp. 510–534.

Zhang, C., & Hung, H. C. (2012). Later hunter-gatherers in southern China, 18000–3000 BC. *Antiquity*, 86(331), 11–29.

Zhang, J., Chen, F., Holmes, J. A. et al. (2011). Holocene monsoon climate documented by oxygen and carbon isotopes from lake sediments and peat bogs in China: A review and synthesis. *Quaternary Science Reviews*, 30 (15–16), 1973–1987.

Zhang, J., Storozum, M. J., Chen, W. et al. (2023). Climatic shifts, geomorphic change, ancient routes of migration and adaption in southwestern China: Site formation processes at Luojiaba, Sichuan Province. *Geoarchaeology*, 38(3), 351–370.

Zhang, J., Zhang, X., Xia, Z., Xu, H., & Zhao, H. (2019). Geomorphic changes along the Yiluo River influenced the emergence of the first urban center at the Erlitou Site, Central Plains of China. *Quaternary International*, 521, 90–103.

Zhang, S., Zhang, J., Zhao, H., Liu, X., & Chen, F. (2020). Spatiotemporal complexity of the 'Greatest Lake Period' in the Tibetan Plateau. *Science Bulletin*, 65(16), 1317–1319.

Zhang, X., Dalrymple, R. W., Yang, S. Y., Lin, C. M., & Wang, P. (2015). Provenance of Holocene sediments in the outer part of the paleo-Qiantang River estuary, China. *Marine Geology*, 366, 1–15.

Zhang, Y., Huang, C. C., Shulmeister, J. et al. (2019). Formation and evolution of the Holocene massive landslide-dammed lakes in the Jishixia Gorges along the upper Yellow River: No relation to China's Great Flood and the Xia Dynasty. *Quaternary Science Reviews*, 218, 267–280.

Zhang, Z., Liu, J., Chen, J. et al. (2021). Holocene climatic optimum in the East Asian monsoon region of China defined by climatic stability. *Earth-Science Reviews*, 212, 103450.

Zhao, C., Liu, Z., Rohling, E. J. et al. (2017). Holocene temperature fluctuations in the northern Tibetan Plateau. *Quaternary Research*, 80(1), 55–65.

Zhao, C., Mo, D., Jin, Y. et al. (2022). A 7000-year record of environmental change: Evolution of Holocene environment and human activities in the Hangjiahu Plain, the lower Yangtze, China. *Geoarchaeology*, 38(3), 335–350.

Zhao, H., Huang, C. C., Wang, H. et al. (2018). Mid-late Holocene temperature and precipitation variations in the Guanting Basin, upper reaches of the Yellow River. *Quaternary International*, 490, 74–81.

Zheng, T., Lei, S., Wang, Z. et al. (2023). Prehistoric sea-salt manufacture as an adaptation strategy to coastal flooding in East China. *Quaternary Science Reviews*, 302, 107966.

Zhuang, Y., Zhang, H., Fang, Y., & Wang, H. (2017). Life cycle of a moat: A detailed micromorphological examination and broader geoarchaeological survey at the late Neolithic Wadian site, Central China. *Journal of Archaeological Science: Reports*, 12, 699–711.

Zhuang, Y., Zhang, X., & Xu, J. (2023). Aquatic landscape and the emergence of walled sites in late Neolithic Central Plains of China: Integrating archaeological and geoarchaeological evidence from the Guchengzhai site. *Archaeological Research in Asia*, 33, 100428.

Zong, Y. (2004). Mid-Holocene sea-level highstand along the Southeast Coast of China. *Quaternary International*, 117(1), 55–67.

Zong, Y., Huang, G., Switzer, A. D., Yu, F., & Yim, W. S. (2009). An evolutionary model for the Holocene formation of the Pearl River delta, China. *The Holocene*, 19(1), 129–142.

Zong, Y., Wang, Z., Innes, J. B., & Chen, Z. (2012). Holocene environmental change and Neolithic rice agriculture in the lower Yangtze region of China: A review. *The Holocene*, 22(6), 623–635.

Zong, Y., Zheng, Z., Huang, K. *et al.* (2013). Changes in sea level, water salinity and wetland habitat linked to the late agricultural development in the Pearl River delta plain of China. *Quaternary Science Reviews*, 70, 145–157.

Acknowledgements

I wish to thank professors Rowan Flad and Erica Brindley for their patience and support and the two reviewers' helpful comments. My sincere thanks also go to Professor Jessica Rawson, Dr. Mike Carson, and Dr. Michael Storozum, who read the draft of this monograph, and Miss Ye Li (PKU PhD candidate), who helped prepare most figures. Miss Chunxia Li (PKU PhD candidate) also helped with preparing the table. I also thank Merton College for hosting me whilst most of this book was written.

Ancient East Asia

Erica Fox Brindley
Pennsylvania State University

Erica Fox Brindley is Professor and Head in the Department of Asian Studies at Pennsylvania State University. She is the author of three books, co-editor of several volumes, and the recipient of the ACLS Ryskamp Fellowship and Humboldt Fellowship. Her research focuses on the history of the self, knowledge, music, and identity in ancient China, as well as on the history of the Yue/Viet cultures from southern China and Vietnam.

Rowan Kimon Flad
Harvard University

Rowan Kimon Flad is the John E. Hudson Professor of Archaeology in the Department of Anthropology at Harvard University. He has authored two books and over 50 articles, edited several volumes, and served as editor of *Asian Perspectives*. His archaeological research focuses on economic and ritual activity, interregional interaction, and technological and environmental change, in the late Neolithic and early Bronze Ages of the Sichuan Basin and the Upper Yellow River valley regions of China.

About the Series

Elements in Ancient East Asia contains multi-disciplinary contributions focusing on the history and culture of East Asia in ancient times. Its framework extends beyond anachronistic, nation-based conceptions of the past, following instead the contours of Asian sub-regions and their interconnections with each other. Within the series there are five thematic groups: 'Sources', which includes excavated texts and other new sources of data; 'Environments', exploring interaction zones of ancient East Asia and long-distance connections; 'Institutions', including the state and its military; 'People', including family, gender, class, and the individual and 'Ideas', concerning religion and philosophy, as well as the arts and sciences. The series presents the latest findings and strikingly new perspectives on the ancient world in East Asia.

Cambridge Elements ≡

Ancient East Asia

Printed in the United States
by Baker & Taylor Publisher Services